# The Anger Management Self-Help Book for Women

CRAFTED BY SKRIUWER

**Copyright © 2024 by Skriuwer.**

All rights reserved. No part of this book may be used or reproduced in any form whatsoever without written permission except in the case of brief quotations in critical articles or reviews.

For more information, contact : **kontakt@skriuwer.com** (www.skriuwer.com)

# TABLE OF CONTENTS

## CHAPTER 1: UNDERSTANDING ANGER IN WOMEN

- *Recognizing hidden versus open anger*
- *Seeing how social pressures shape anger*
- *Noticing early physical signs of anger*

## CHAPTER 2: FINDING THE REASONS BEHIND ANGER

- *Identifying personal anger triggers*
- *Uncovering deeper emotions under anger*
- *Learning to observe patterns from the past*

## CHAPTER 3: PHYSICAL & EMOTIONAL EFFECTS OF ANGER

- *Understanding how anger affects the body*
- *Exploring stress hormones and tension*
- *Linking chronic anger to health problems*

## CHAPTER 4: HOW ANGER AFFECTS RELATIONSHIPS

- *Noticing anger's impact on trust and closeness*
- *Addressing anger-driven conflicts with loved ones*
- *Finding healthier ways to communicate needs*

## CHAPTER 5: SAFE WAYS TO EXPRESS ANGER

- *Channeling anger into non-harmful outlets*
- *Practicing calm methods like writing or physical activity*
- *Releasing tension without damaging relationships*

## CHAPTER 6: BUILDING SELF-AWARENESS

- *Observing thought patterns and body cues*
- *Creating a journal or log to track triggers*
- *Spotting early anger signs to act quickly*

---

## CHAPTER 7: LEARNING BETTER COMMUNICATION

- *Using "I" statements to reduce blame*
- *Listening actively to defuse tension*
- *Maintaining respect even in heated talks*

---

## CHAPTER 8: WAYS TO SOLVE CONFLICTS

- *Applying structured steps for resolution*
- *Finding compromise or collaboration*
- *Keeping anger from overshadowing problems*

---

## CHAPTER 9: HANDLING STRESS AND ANGER

- *Recognizing stress as a root cause*
- *Reducing daily stressors to lower anger risk*
- *Maintaining health through rest and balance*

---

## CHAPTER 10: MANAGING RESPONSIBILITIES AND ANGER

- *Avoiding overload that sparks frustration*
- *Delegating tasks and setting priorities*
- *Finding personal time to recharge*

## CHAPTER 11: MOVING PAST GUILT AND SHAME

- *Distinguishing guilt from shame*
- *Understanding how shame fuels anger*
- *Using self-compassion to break negative cycles*

## CHAPTER 12: RAISING CONFIDENCE AND SELF-WORTH

- *Building a sense of value to handle anger*
- *Shifting self-talk from harsh to supportive*
- *Setting boundaries guided by self-respect*

## CHAPTER 13: DEALING WITH ANGER IN THE WORKPLACE

- *Spotting triggers at the office or job site*
- *Keeping composure with colleagues or bosses*
- *Balancing productivity with emotional well-being*

## CHAPTER 14: HELPING FAMILY AND FRIENDS UNDERSTAND

- *Explaining anger's roots to loved ones*
- *Asking for healthy support or space*
- *Preventing misunderstandings about anger issues*

## CHAPTER 15: CHANGING NEGATIVE THOUGHTS INTO POSITIVE ONES

- *Identifying negative thinking patterns*
- *Replacing harsh internal talk with balanced views*
- *Overcoming all-or-nothing and mind-reading habits*

## CHAPTER 16: RELAXATION METHODS FOR ANGER CONTROL

- Practicing deep breathing and muscle relaxation
- Using grounding exercises to stay present
- Applying quick calm-down techniques on the go

## CHAPTER 17: AVOIDING COMMON ANGER TRIGGERS

- Recognizing personal environmental triggers
- Reducing exposure to stressful situations
- Adapting routines to prevent frequent flare-ups

## CHAPTER 18: RELEASING ANGER THROUGH FORGIVENESS

- Understanding forgiveness as personal freedom
- Separating forgiveness from excusing harmful acts
- Finding emotional relief by letting go of grudges

## CHAPTER 19: STAYING CALM IN PUBLIC SETTINGS

- Coping with crowds, delays, and rude strangers
- Applying subtle techniques to lower stress
- Exiting tense situations with dignity

## CHAPTER 20: MAKING LONG-LASTING CHANGES

- Integrating anger management into daily habits
- Handling setbacks and continuing growth
- Maintaining healthier responses for the future

# Chapter 1: Understanding Anger in Women

Anger is a normal feeling. It shows that something in your life is making you feel upset or hurt. Anger can help you become aware that a situation might be unfair or painful for you. Many times, people think that anger is always a bad thing, but that is not true. Anger can be healthy when it helps you stand up for yourself or protect someone who is in danger. However, anger can become a problem when it causes harm to yourself or others. In this chapter, we will look at anger as it relates to women and how it can shape thoughts, actions, and health in day-to-day life.

When you think of anger, you might picture someone shouting, slamming doors, or saying hurtful words. But anger can also be hidden. A woman might feel a pounding in her chest but never show it. She might feel shaky hands or a knot in her stomach without raising her voice. She might smile on the outside but feel a lot of rage on the inside. It is important to understand that anger is not one simple feeling. It can come out in many ways, and each person has a unique way of expressing it or holding it in.

One reason anger can feel different for women is the pressure to seem calm or polite at all times. Some people might say that it looks bad for a woman to be angry, or that a woman who shows anger is behaving in a wrong way. Because of these ideas, a woman might try to hide or bury her anger. She might blame herself for feeling that emotion, thinking that it is shameful or unladylike. Over time, this can cause her anger to grow inside. Instead of letting it out in a safe way, she might push it down until it explodes or affects her body in unhealthy ways.

Hiding anger can also lead to confusion. A woman may feel guilty that she gets angry about things that may seem small, like a family member speaking in a harsh tone, a co-worker taking credit for her work, or a friend arriving late. She might ask herself, "Why am I angry?" or "Is it wrong for me to feel this way?" These doubts can make her feel alone. She might worry that nobody understands, so she chooses to stay quiet.

In the past, many people thought of anger as a feeling that men had more often. Some said that men had a right to get angry, while women were expected to smile and not cause trouble. This way of thinking put pressure on women. They had fewer safe places to speak about their angry feelings, so they got used to holding them inside. This can lead to a cycle of anger, sadness, and maybe even shame.

It is helpful to see anger as a message. Picture it as a little alarm that rings in your head when you notice that something feels off. You can either ignore the alarm, or you can try to figure out why it is ringing. If you keep ignoring the alarm, you might start feeling stressed, tired, or frustrated. You might start feeling tension in your body, like headaches or muscle aches. Or, you might feel withdrawn and not want to see friends or family. By answering this alarm, you can take a closer look at what is going on and make a plan to handle things in a healthier way.

Women can face anger for a number of reasons. Some might be tied to life events. For instance, a woman who is under a lot of stress at work might be more on edge. She might feel that her boss does not respect her time, or that her coworkers do not value her opinions. She might also be trying to balance responsibilities at home, like cooking, cleaning, and caring for children. If she feels that no one is helping her, or that people expect too much from her, anger may rise. In addition, some women face problems like unfair pay or discrimination, and these issues can create a sense of anger that feels hard to manage.

It is also important to think about how anger can affect a woman's body. When you feel angry, your body goes through changes. Your heart may beat faster, your muscles may tense up, and your mind might become more alert. This is often called the "fight or flight" response. It is a survival mechanism that helps you act quickly when you sense danger. However, if you stay in this high-alert state for too long, it can harm your health. You may start to experience chronic stress, trouble sleeping, or high blood pressure.

Emotional effects of anger can be just as serious. Long-term anger can damage your mood and cause problems like sadness or worry. You might feel guilty about being angry, and this guilt can weigh you down. Also, if anger leads you to say or do hurtful things, you may feel regret later. This can create a loop of angry feelings followed by shame, which can make you want to avoid facing your anger. You might act like nothing is wrong, even though you feel tense or upset inside.

It is also good to note that there are different ways to express anger. Some ways are obvious, like yelling or throwing things. But other ways are less direct. Some people use sarcasm or make rude comments to show anger. Others might pull away from people or give them the silent treatment. These are all signs that the person is upset. When you see these signs in yourself, it is important not to judge yourself too harshly. Instead, you can learn to see these signs as hints that you need a healthier way to let out your feelings.

In many cases, anger happens alongside other feelings. You might feel disappointed, embarrassed, or jealous. You might feel fear or sadness. Anger can stand out more than these feelings, because it often feels more powerful. It can even hide those softer feelings, making it hard to know what is actually going on inside. By understanding the main emotion behind the anger, you can find a clearer way to deal with the real problem.

Sometimes, people think that anger must always be loud. They expect it to come in the form of a scream or a strong outburst. But quiet anger can be just as serious. A woman who holds her anger inside might stew over it. She might feel hurt or resentful for a long time without ever saying a word. This can hurt relationships and cause misunderstandings. It can also harm her sense of self-esteem, as she might start thinking that her needs do not matter.

When a woman understands her anger, she can begin to make choices that are healthier. She can learn methods to calm down before she reaches a boiling point. She can recognize when her body is telling her she is upset, such as feeling her shoulders tighten or her face become hot. By noticing these signs, she can choose to pause and breathe, instead of acting without thinking.

Understanding anger also means letting go of shame. Being angry does not mean you are a bad person. Anger is a normal reaction to something that feels wrong or unfair. If you call yourself a bad person for being angry, you might miss a chance to fix the problem. Instead, you can see anger as a clue that can lead to real change. Once you recognize it, you can decide how to act in a way that will help you and those around you.

It may help to think about how you learned to handle anger as a child. Maybe you saw someone in your family who exploded with rage whenever they were upset. Or maybe you grew up in a home where no one talked about anger at all. These early life experiences can shape how you see anger as an adult. If you learned that anger is scary or shameful, you might want to hide it. If you saw someone lash out in anger, you might think that is the only way to respond. The good news is that even if you learned unhealthy ways, you can still discover better ways to handle anger now.

Another factor that affects anger in women is the role of hormones. Women go through hormonal changes during their monthly cycles, during pregnancy, and at other times in life. These changes can make mood shifts feel more intense. While it is not correct to say that hormones are the main cause of anger, they can affect how strong anger feels or how quickly it builds. It can help to track these patterns, but it is also important not to blame everything on hormones. Anger can still be managed, even if it feels stronger at certain times.

Gender roles and expectations also contribute. Women often learn to be caretakers or supporters in their families, which can put extra pressure on them. If a woman feels like she has to care for everyone else first, she may forget her own needs. This can build tension and resentment. Over time, this resentment might become anger. Sometimes, this anger is not even noticed until it erupts. Recognizing these patterns can help a woman find new ways to set boundaries and look after herself.

It is also worth pointing out that anger can come from feeling trapped or powerless. For example, if a woman is not treated fairly at work, or if she has a partner who does not respect her, she might feel that she has no say in the situation. This feeling of powerlessness can make her angry, even if she does not show it. She might feel that talking about it will lead nowhere. But in truth, speaking up can be a step toward finding a solution. If she never says anything, the anger remains inside, causing her distress.

Relationships can also be shaped by anger. If a friend or partner treats you poorly, it is natural to feel upset. The question is how you handle that feeling. Do you speak up, or do you let it build? If you keep quiet, you may feel angry that you never had a chance to share your feelings. On the other hand, if you yell or say mean things, the other person might shut down or feel attacked. Neither extreme is helpful. Balance is possible, but it takes understanding and practice.

In summary, anger in women can be shaped by many factors: social pressures, past experiences, hidden feelings, and physical changes in the body. Anger is not always wrong. It can be a sign that something needs attention. By noticing anger in ourselves, we can start to make choices about how to respond. We can take steps to speak up for ourselves, respect our boundaries, and stay healthy both inside and out.

In this book, you will learn more about how to deal with anger in a safer way. Anger does not have to ruin your relationships or harm your health. With proper tools, it can be handled in a way that helps you build a better life. The next chapter will focus on finding the reasons behind anger. It will help you look deeper into where anger starts and how you can learn from it. Keep in mind that knowledge is a powerful first step. When you understand your anger, you have a better chance of using it in a way that helps rather than harms.

# Chapter 2: Finding the Reasons Behind Anger

Anger does not happen for no reason. Even if it feels sudden, there is almost always something behind it. The reasons can vary from person to person. For one woman, it might be stress at work. For another, it might be arguments at home. Some people might be upset by unfair treatment, lack of respect, or feeling left out. Sometimes, the triggers are big, such as facing discrimination or going through a divorce. Other times, they are small, like someone cutting in line or a friend forgetting to call.

In order to handle anger in a healthy way, you need to understand what sets it off. This can be tricky because anger can hide other feelings. You might feel disappointed, scared, or hurt, but anger comes out on the surface. By looking closer at these hidden layers, you can better understand your triggers. Then you can deal with the true source of the problem instead of just the angry reaction.

One common source of anger is feeling that others do not take you seriously. For example, if you speak up in a meeting at work and your boss talks over you, you might feel hurt and undervalued. You might also feel that it is unfair. Your anger might come from a place of wanting respect. In a family setting, you might feel that relatives do not appreciate your help or that they ignore your boundaries. You may notice that small comments they make light a fuse inside you. Those comments might seem harmless to them, but to you, they can feel like proof that they do not respect you.

Unresolved problems from the past can also cause anger. If you had a rough childhood, you might carry around feelings that are waiting to come out. For instance, if you grew up with a parent who belittled you, you might now get angry when someone criticizes you. This is because those old wounds are still sensitive. You might think that you are simply reacting to the present moment, but the real reason goes back to earlier experiences. Recognizing this can help you see that your anger might be bigger than the current situation. It is like having a bruise that hurts more if someone accidentally touches it.

Stress is another factor. When you have too many duties or too little time, even a small annoyance can feel huge. You might snap at a friend or loved one for something minor. Then you wonder, "Why did I get so angry over that?" The answer might be that you are already under pressure. Any added problem can push you over the edge. That is why, if you want to handle anger, you need to manage your stress levels too. Cutting down on stressors can lower the heat beneath your anger.

Feeling that things are unfair is a powerful trigger for anger. This can happen in relationships, work environments, or society in general. If you see that someone gets special treatment while you work twice as hard, you might feel angry. If you notice that your boss always listens to a certain coworker but not you, you can feel slighted. If you experience or witness something that goes against your sense of right and wrong, you might react with anger. That anger can be a sign that you value fairness and justice. It can also motivate you to speak up or make changes.

Fear is another reason behind anger. You might feel scared about losing someone you love or worried about failing at a task. That fear can turn into anger as a defense. If you feel that someone is threatening something you care about, you might get angry in an attempt to protect it. In some cases, anger can be a cover for fear because anger feels stronger or safer than admitting you are scared. But recognizing that fear can help you address the real concern.

Sometimes, anger comes from a lack of personal space or time for yourself. Women often have many roles: mother, daughter, friend, partner, worker. They might find themselves always helping others and never taking a break. This can cause built-up frustration. A woman might explode in anger because she feels that no one is giving her the room to rest or recharge. Identifying this trigger means learning to set limits and communicate your needs to others.

Past heartbreak can also play a part. If you have been hurt by someone you trusted, you might carry anger as a layer of protection. You might feel ready to snap at the smallest sign of betrayal. This can harm new relationships. You might push people away or blame them for what happened in the past. Understanding this pattern can help you see that your anger in the present might be fueled by old wounds. It also reminds you to seek healing for those earlier hurts.

Cultural or social expectations can lead to anger too. If your upbringing taught you that certain things must be done in certain ways, you might get upset if people do not follow those unwritten rules. You might hold onto anger because the real conflict is between your beliefs and someone else's actions. But if you do not examine these beliefs, you may not realize why you are so upset. By asking yourself, "Why do I believe this is the only way?" or "Why does this bother me so much?" you can uncover hidden causes of your anger.

Sometimes, anger is related to feeling let down. If a close friend promised to help you with something important but did not show up, you might feel abandoned. If a family member agreed to be supportive in a project but then forgot, you might feel alone. This sense of feeling let down can build over time, especially if it happens again and again. Anger rises because you do not feel that the other person cares about your needs as much as you care about theirs.

There can also be a clash of personal values. For instance, if you value honesty and you discover that someone lied to you, you could feel furious. Or if you respect kindness and see someone acting cruelly, you might be filled with anger. These strong emotions come from the fact that someone went against something you hold dear. By recognizing that your core values are being challenged, you can see why your anger feels so strong.

Another important factor is comparison. Women might compare themselves to others who seem to have everything under control. Social media can feed these feelings. If you see pictures of people who appear happy, successful, and calm, you might get angry with yourself for not meeting those standards. Or you might get angry at society for promoting unrealistic images. This anger can be directed inward, causing low self-esteem, or outward, causing frustration with the world around you. Understanding this trigger can help you remember that everyone has problems, and that social media does not always show the full truth.

Finding the reasons behind your anger requires honest self-reflection. One practical way to do this is to keep a simple log. Each time you notice anger, write down what happened just before you got mad. Note what was said or done, who was involved, and how you felt physically. Did your heart race? Did your cheeks get hot? Did your hands shake? Then jot down how you responded. Did you yell, stay silent, or walk away? Over time, patterns will appear. You may see that certain people or situations always set you off. You may realize that you usually get angry when you are already tired or hungry. You might notice that certain words or behaviors from others trigger an old pain.

By gathering this information, you can start to see your anger as a signal rather than a mystery. You might realize that you have certain "anger hot spots" in your life. For example, maybe you feel especially upset about being disrespected at work because you felt overlooked as a child. Or maybe loud noises bother you deeply because they remind you of arguments from your past. By seeing these deeper reasons, you can take steps to deal with them in a healthy way. You might talk to a counselor or friend about how to cope with old hurts. You might practice self-care or set boundaries when you feel your stress level rising.

Some people worry that if they look too deeply at the reasons for their anger, they will become overwhelmed by sadness or regret. In fact, understanding the root cause of anger can reduce those heavy feelings. When you see why you are angry, you can begin to address those needs. You can work on healing old emotional wounds. You can make changes in your present life so that the same triggers do not keep popping up. Though it might feel uncomfortable at first, this process can help you gain a sense of control over your emotions.

It is also worth noting that some triggers might be outside of your control. For example, you might be angry about a problem in society, such as unfair treatment of women in certain places or roles. You might feel helpless to change this right away. However, understanding that this is a trigger for you can still help. You can decide how you want to respond. Perhaps you choose to share your thoughts with people in your life. Perhaps you find a safe space to volunteer or do something that feels meaningful to you. The key is to see that you are reacting because you have strong values and beliefs, and you want the world to be fair and kind.

You might also find that some reasons for anger are tied to your self-talk. Self-talk is the voice in your mind that comments on what happens. If this voice is harsh or critical, it can make you angrier. For example, if you make a small mistake and your inner voice says, "You are useless," you might get angry at yourself, or even lash out at others. By changing how you talk to yourself, you can reduce these angry flare-ups. Instead of saying, "I am a failure," you can say, "I made a mistake, but I can learn from it."

In some cases, medical or mental health conditions can play a role in anger. For instance, depression and anxiety can include irritability. If you notice that you are always on edge and angry, it might be worth talking to a professional. Sometimes, treating an underlying condition can help with anger issues as well. This does not mean that your anger is "all in your head." Rather, it is a sign that your emotional health might need extra care.

It is also wise to consider how physical health can affect anger. When you are tired, hungry, or ill, you may be more likely to snap. Think about how children act when they need a nap or a snack. They might throw tantrums because they cannot handle their discomfort. Adults can feel this way too, even if we do not realize it. Taking care of our bodies by getting enough sleep, eating balanced meals, and staying active can lower the chance of anger taking over.

To keep track of the reasons behind your anger, you can ask yourself simple questions: "What am I really upset about?" "Was there something that happened earlier that is affecting me now?" "Is there another feeling behind this anger, like fear or sadness?" "Am I hungry, tired, or stressed?" By making these questions a habit, you can begin to see anger as a clue about what is going on inside you.

Finding the reasons behind anger does not mean you ignore the anger or push it away. It means you learn from it. You notice that anger is telling you something. If you pay attention, you might find that you need to stand up for yourself, set a boundary, or ask for help. In other cases, you might discover that you are upset because of fear, grief, or feelings of not being good enough. Recognizing these feelings can guide you toward healthier ways of dealing with them.

Anger can be like a locked box. From the outside, it seems like pure rage. But when you open the box, you might find pain, loneliness, or other deep emotions that have not been addressed. By opening that box and looking at what is inside, you can begin to work on real solutions. This is often the most important step in managing anger—figuring out what is at its core. Once you do that, your anger will no longer be an unexplainable force.

As we move forward in this book, keep in mind that anger, while at times overwhelming, can be handled in a calmer way. You do not have to be at the mercy of flare-ups that come out of nowhere. By finding the reasons behind your anger, you give yourself a chance to change how you respond. You become more aware of the signals your mind and body send you. You gain more say in how you act when that heat builds in your chest. This is a step toward a life that feels balanced and clear.

# Chapter 3: Physical and Emotional Effects of Anger

Anger can feel like a sudden wave in your body, or it can creep up slowly until you notice tension in your muscles or a knot in your stomach. When women experience anger, it can affect the body and mind in ways that are not always obvious. It can lead to short-term issues, like a racing heartbeat, but it can also create long-lasting problems if it goes unchecked. In this chapter, we will look closely at the physical and emotional effects of anger. We will also consider how these effects may harm your well-being if you do not find ways to handle anger in a healthier manner.

---

## Recognizing Physical Signs

The body reacts to anger by preparing itself for a threat. This comes from a survival response that is rooted in our biology. Thousands of years ago, people needed to be ready to fight or run if they were in danger. While life has changed in many ways, our bodies still hold onto this response. When you feel anger, your body may do several things:

1. **Speed up Your Heart Rate**: The heart may start beating faster, pumping more blood to your muscles. This is part of the body's way of getting you ready to act if you need to.
2. **Release Stress Hormones**: Substances like adrenaline and cortisol can surge through your body. These hormones give you energy in the short term, but they can be harmful if they remain at high levels for too long.
3. **Tighten Your Muscles**: You might feel yourself clenching your jaw or making fists without noticing. Your shoulders might rise, or your neck might grow stiff. These are natural ways the body gets ready to protect itself.
4. **Change Your Breathing**: When anger spikes, you might breathe more quickly or hold your breath for a moment. This can leave you feeling lightheaded or tense.
5. **Raise Your Body Temperature**: Some people feel a surge of heat when anger strikes. You might notice your face getting warm or your palms sweating.

These physical signs are not bad in and of themselves. They are normal responses to a strong feeling. The problem is that many women have these reactions often, without finding a safe release. If your heart races and your muscles tighten every time you face a trigger, it can wear down your body over time.

---

## Lasting Physical Problems

When anger is left unresolved, these physical signs can grow into long-term problems. For instance, if your body often releases stress hormones without proper relief, you might face the following issues:

1. **High Blood Pressure**: Repeated spikes in stress hormones can strain your heart and blood vessels, which might raise your blood pressure. Over time, this can put you at risk for heart disease or other health troubles.
2. **Tension Headaches or Migraines**: Constant muscle tightness in your neck and shoulders can cause headaches. If you already get migraines, anger might make them worse or happen more often.
3. **Trouble Sleeping**: When anger keeps your mind racing, it can be hard to fall asleep or stay asleep. Poor sleep can lead to low energy, poor concentration, and more mood swings.
4. **Weakened Immune System**: Long-term stress can affect how well your body fights off illnesses. You might notice that you get sick more often or take longer to recover.
5. **Digestive Problems**: Some people feel queasy or have stomach cramps when angry. If this happens a lot, it can upset the balance in your digestive system, leading to ongoing discomfort or even ulcers in severe cases.

Not everyone who feels anger will develop these health problems, but the risk is higher if you handle anger by holding it in or letting it simmer too often. The body needs periods of calm to restore balance. If the stress response is always turned on, you cannot fully relax.

## Emotional Effects

Anger does not only affect the body. It can also shape how you think and feel. Some women might describe feeling a heavy cloud of resentment or a nagging sense of irritability. Others might feel a sudden flash of rage, followed by guilt. Still others might experience shame for being upset, or confusion about why they are upset at all.

Below are some common emotional effects of anger:

1. **Shame and Guilt**: You might feel bad about being angry, especially if you think anger is an unworthy emotion. You might worry you are causing trouble for people around you, or that you are failing to keep your composure.
2. **Isolation**: If you find yourself getting upset regularly, you might pull away from friends or family, fearing that your anger will harm those relationships. Over time, you might feel alone because you have less contact with people you care about.
3. **Low Self-Esteem**: Constant anger can lead you to think poorly of yourself. You might blame yourself for not being able to stay calm. You might believe you are an angry person by nature, rather than seeing anger as a signal about a deeper problem.
4. **Mood Swings**: Anger can shift quickly to sadness or frustration. You might find yourself crying after a burst of anger, or feeling hopeless once your anger cools. These mood swings can be tough to manage, especially if you do not understand why they happen.
5. **Difficulty Focusing**: Feeling on edge can make it hard to concentrate on daily tasks. You might make mistakes at work, forget important appointments, or struggle to keep track of simple details.

When you are stuck in cycles of anger, your emotional health can go downhill. You might feel as if you are walking on a tightrope, ready to snap at any small annoyance. This can lead you to see the world as a harsh place, where you are always waiting for the next problem. Recognizing these emotional effects can be a wake-up call. It might push you to learn healthier ways of dealing with anger before it sets deeper roots in your life.

## Feelings That Hide Under Anger

Anger is often a cover for other feelings. If you look closely, you might find sadness, fear, grief, or even longing. Anger might feel more powerful than these gentler emotions, so it takes the spotlight. You might see this in situations where you lash out at someone, only to realize later that you were actually scared or disappointed.

By understanding the emotions that live beneath anger, you can handle the real source of the problem. For example, if you are angry at a friend for not calling you back, you might realize that you feel hurt or lonely. Anger appears on the surface, but the main issue is that you crave reassurance or support. If you focus only on the angry outburst, you might never get what you truly need: a sense of closeness or understanding.

---

## How Anger Impacts Mental Health

Some people think of anger as an emotion separate from sadness or worry. However, anger can play a big role in mental health. A woman who is angry all the time might also be feeling depressed. She might lose interest in things she once enjoyed. Or she might have anxiety about when anger will strike next, which could lead to panic attacks.

Anger can feed negative thought patterns. You might start to believe that no one cares or that problems will never get better. This can make you more irritable. Over time, you could find yourself trapped in a cycle of anger and hopelessness. That is why it is important to notice signs of deeper emotional distress, such as trouble sleeping, changes in appetite, or constant worry. Sometimes, when anger and other concerns build up, talking to a counselor or therapist can help you unpack the layers and find solutions.

---

## Short-Term vs. Long-Term Effects

It can help to divide the effects of anger into short-term and long-term. In the short term, anger might make your blood pressure go up, or make you shout at someone who upset you. But if that anger is brief and you find a quick, healthy way to calm down, the damage may be small. You might feel bad afterward, but the event passes, and life goes on.

Long-term anger is more harmful. It can become a pattern that shapes your daily life. You might begin each day feeling tense, as if you are already bracing yourself for trouble. Your muscles might stay tight for hours, leading to soreness or chronic pain. Your thoughts might turn negative, making it hard to trust the people around you. This kind of simmering anger can push away friends, strain family ties, or even affect job performance.

Many women do not realize that their bodies and minds are stuck in a pattern of chronic anger or stress. They might assume that it is normal to have headaches every day or to feel shaky after a disagreement. It is not normal to live in that constant state of unrest. Learning to recognize the difference between a brief spike of anger and a lasting anger pattern can help you decide what steps you need to take.

---

## Impact on Daily Behavior

Another sign of anger's effects can be changes in how you behave day to day. You might notice that:

1. **You Snap at Loved Ones More Easily**: Small comments can set you off, leading to arguments that seem bigger than they should be.
2. **You Avoid Activities**: You might skip social events or even errands because you do not want to face situations that could upset you.
3. **You Engage in Risky Behavior**: Anger can push some people to seek quick relief, perhaps through harmful habits.
4. **You Bottle Up Feelings**: If you are afraid of what might happen if you show anger, you might stuff it down. This can lead to resentment that builds over time.

These behaviors can become habits. For example, if you fear that your anger will make you lose control, you might avoid conflicts, never share your feelings, and distance yourself from people. This avoidance can make you feel lonely, while your hidden anger still lurks inside.

## Anger and Relationships with Yourself

Anger does not just affect how you treat others. It can shape how you treat yourself. When you are angry often, you might be harsh on yourself. You might judge every mistake, big or small, and blame yourself for not being perfect. This can harm your sense of self-worth, leading you to feel like you cannot do anything right.

Some women might direct the anger inward, which can look like self-punishment. They might avoid seeking help because they think they do not deserve it. Or they might overwork themselves, thinking that they have to prove something to the world. In other cases, they might neglect their health, such as by not eating properly or avoiding medical checkups.

When you are constantly upset, it is easy to overlook the need for rest and care. You might think, "I do not have time to relax," or "I do not deserve a break." In the end, this kind of harsh self-treatment only feeds the cycle of anger, because you remain in a state of tension and frustration.

---

## The Role of Thoughts

Anger often begins with thoughts. For example, you might see someone cut in front of you in a line. The thought pops up: "They are so rude. They are disrespecting me on purpose." That thought can trigger anger. If you keep having thoughts like these, your anger can grow.

Your inner voice also plays a role. If your self-talk is critical, you might assume that others are treating you poorly on purpose or that nothing ever works out. When an event happens, you might jump to negative conclusions. If you can learn to pause and question your thoughts, you might catch these patterns before they turn into full-blown anger.

You can ask yourself: "Is there proof that this person wanted to hurt me?" or "Could there be another reason for what just happened?" This does not mean you ignore rude behavior; it just helps you respond in a calmer way. It also helps you see that not every event is a personal attack.

---

## Emotional Exhaustion

When anger becomes a regular part of life, you may experience emotional exhaustion. This is a state where you feel drained, as if you have nothing left to give. You might be tired in the morning even after a full night's sleep. Small tasks can feel overwhelming.

Emotional exhaustion can make your anger outbursts more frequent. You might not have the energy to hold back, so you lash out without thinking. This can cause guilt or shame, which then leads to more exhaustion. Recognizing this pattern can help you realize that you need real rest, both physically and emotionally.

---

## Impact on Confidence

Repeated anger can lower confidence. Each time you lose your temper, you might feel you have failed in some way. You might worry what others think of you or fear that you cannot control your feelings. If you end up saying hurtful things in the heat of the moment, you might feel even less confident later, because you regret your actions.

Over time, you might come to believe that you are not capable of handling pressure. You might shy away from challenges at work or in your personal life. This can hold you back from reaching goals or creating strong connections with others. By noticing how anger affects your confidence, you can see why it is so important to find methods that prevent anger from taking over.

---

## Harm to Your Sense of Peace

When anger rules your life, it can feel like peace is impossible to find. Even if you have quiet moments, you might still feel uneasy. You might replay arguments in your mind, thinking about what you could have said or done differently. This mental replay keeps you stuck in anger, preventing you from enjoying calm times.

Inner peace does not mean you never get angry. It means knowing how to handle that anger when it comes up. But if anger is a regular visitor in your day, you might not remember what peace feels like. It is important to recognize that true peace involves giving yourself permission to step away from the cycle of anger, regret, and self-judgment.

---

## The Challenge of Changing Old Patterns

Some women have lived with anger for so long that it feels like a natural part of who they are. Changing that can feel scary or even impossible. They might have tried calming methods that did not work immediately, or they might have grown used to dealing with life through anger.

But realizing the effects of anger on your body and mind is often the first step. This awareness can give you a reason to try again or to try something new. It can help you see that anger is affecting your health, your mood, and your relationships. This knowledge is not meant to scare you—it is meant to show you that you have the power to do something about it.

---

## Breaking the Cycle

Understanding the effects of anger is not just about listing problems. It also helps you see what you stand to gain by making changes. If you lower your anger levels, you might sleep better, have fewer headaches, and feel calmer around the people you love. You might find that you can concentrate on your work or hobbies without the weight of anger pressing on your mind.

Breaking the cycle does not happen overnight. It may involve learning new ways to react when you feel the early signs of anger. It may require talking to a counselor or finding safe outlets for your emotions, such as writing or gentle exercise. You might also need to look at the bigger sources of stress in your life. If your job or home situation is pushing you past your limits, reducing anger might mean making a change in those areas if you can.

## Seeking Support

One of the hardest parts of dealing with anger is feeling like you have to manage it by yourself. You might feel embarrassed about your outbursts, or afraid that others will judge you. But seeking support from friends, family, or professionals can lighten the load. Telling someone you trust that you are struggling can remind you that you do not have to face this alone.

Support might also give you a new perspective. Sometimes, an outside view helps you see patterns you did not notice. A friend might point out that you always seem to get angry after long workdays. A therapist might help you dig into the root cause of your anger and teach you ways to relax. The point is that you do not have to remain stuck in the physical and emotional toll that anger creates.

---

## Putting the Pieces Together

Anger can act like a storm passing through your life. After the storm, you might see the wreckage in the form of headaches, poor sleep, strained relationships, or an overall sense that you are not at your best. It can take time to clean up after each storm. If these storms happen often, you might feel you never have a chance to catch your breath.

When you know how anger affects your body and emotions, you are more prepared to spot the warning signs. You can notice when your heart starts racing or when your thoughts turn harsh. This awareness gives you a chance to pause and think about how you want to respond. Instead of letting anger take over, you can practice methods that help you calm down or talk things out in a way that does not harm you or others.

---

## Moving Forward

Anger does not have to rule your life. Even if you have felt angry for years, you can learn healthier responses. It starts with understanding what anger does to your mind and body. From there, you can make new choices about what to do with that feeling when it appears. You can learn to spot the tension in your body, question your thoughts, and find constructive ways to let go of or address your anger.

In the coming chapters, you will read about safe ways to express anger and skills for communication that can help you talk through conflicts. You will also learn how to handle stress, since stress often goes hand in hand with anger. By understanding the physical and emotional effects in detail, you are taking a step toward real change.

Remember: Anger is not just about snapping at someone in the heat of the moment. It can shape your health, mood, and relationships if it is not dealt with. Yet, you hold the power to make different choices once you see the full picture of what anger can do. Keep this in mind as you look toward learning new methods and skills in the next chapters.

# Chapter 4: How Anger Affects Relationships

Relationships are a key part of life, whether they are with partners, children, friends, or coworkers. When anger shows up often, it can strain or weaken these connections. People may shy away from you because they fear a hostile reaction, or they may become hostile themselves, creating a cycle of conflict. In this chapter, we will look closely at the ways anger can shape relationships and what steps you might take to avoid harm to the people you care about.

---

## Anger in Close Relationships

A close relationship could be with a partner, a best friend, or a family member. In these connections, people usually share more time and emotions with one another. When anger flares up, it might feel more intense in these settings than anywhere else. That is because you often expect loved ones to treat you gently and understand you better than others do.

1. **Arguments That Spin Out of Control**: In a heated argument, you might say or hear cruel words that cut deep. Later, both sides might feel guilty or ashamed. These words can linger, and the hurt can build if there is no proper repair afterward.
2. **Silent Treatment**: Some women react to anger by withdrawing rather than yelling. This can leave the other person guessing what is wrong. Over time, lack of communication can push people apart, as misunderstandings add up.
3. **Constant Tension**: If arguments happen often, even small disagreements can stir up anxiety. You might walk on eggshells, afraid that the other person will set you off—or that you will set them off. This creates a lack of safety in the relationship.

When anger becomes a regular part of these close connections, the warmth and trust that once held the bond together may fade. People might still care for each other, but they do not feel calm or safe sharing their feelings. Over time, anger might overshadow positive moments, leaving little room for closeness.

---

## Effects on Friendships

Friends are people you choose to spend time with, but anger can put stress on these bonds as well. Here are some ways anger can creep into friendships:

1. **Jealousy and Anger**: Sometimes anger in friendships grows from comparing yourself to your friends. If your friend has a new job or is spending time with someone else, you might feel left out or jealous, which can turn into anger.
2. **Lack of Patience**: If you are already upset with your own life, you might snap at a friend who makes a harmless comment. This can leave your friend confused or even hurt, damaging trust.
3. **Avoidance**: If you worry that your anger might burst out, you might avoid seeing your friends or replying to their calls. In this way, anger robs you of social support and deepens any loneliness you already feel.

Friends might try to understand and offer help, but if the anger is intense or frequent, they may start to pull back. No matter how strong the bond was, it can weaken if one person's angry behavior overshadows the positive aspects of the friendship.

---

## Parenting and Anger

If you have children, anger can influence how you connect with them. Children learn from what they see. If they see a parent lose control often, they might grow fearful or think that anger is the only way to handle problems. Here are some ways anger can appear in parenting:

1. **Harsh Words or Threats**: In moments of anger, a parent might yell or use scary language. Even if the parent feels regret later, the child might remember the harsh tone.
2. **Inconsistent Limits**: If you set rules for your child but enforce them only when you are mad, the child might learn to behave only when they sense your anger. This can make discipline more about fear rather than understanding.

3. **Emotional Distance**: If a parent bottles up anger, a child might sense something is wrong but not know what it is. This can make the child anxious or unsure how to act around their parent.

It is normal for parents to feel frustration, but if anger is the main response, it can hinder the child's ability to feel safe. Over time, the child might respond with rebellion, fear, or emotional withdrawal. Realizing how anger affects parenting can motivate you to find ways to stay calm, set clearer limits, and talk things through even when you are upset.

## Anger in the Workplace

Work relationships also matter. Anger on the job can lead to conflicts with coworkers or bosses, and it can keep you from doing your best work. For example:

1. **Angry Outbursts**: If you snap at a coworker, you might lose their respect or trust. You might gain a reputation for being difficult, which can affect future promotions or assignments.
2. **Poor Teamwork**: If everyone is on edge, people might be less willing to share ideas or help each other. Anger can block communication, leading to mistakes and resentment.
3. **Stressful Environment**: A workplace where anger is common can become a place people dread. This can raise tension further, making the anger problem worse.

The stress of work can also feed your anger, creating a cycle. You might feel overworked, underpaid, or disrespected. These feelings can build until you lash out. Or you might keep quiet, letting bitterness grow until it affects your performance or mental well-being.

## Common Relationship Patterns Fueled by Anger

Anger can show up in certain patterns across different relationships. Learning these patterns can help you spot issues early:

1. **Blaming and Shaming**: One person might label the other as the sole cause of all problems. This can leave the other person feeling cornered and defensive.
2. **Stonewalling**: A person might refuse to discuss an issue, shutting down communication. This can cause anger in the other person, who might feel ignored or dismissed.
3. **Passive Aggression**: Instead of openly discussing anger, a person might show their feelings in indirect ways, like giving backhanded compliments or subtly sabotaging another's efforts.
4. **Escalation**: Small disagreements can blow up into huge fights if people have built-up anger that has not been addressed.

Recognizing these patterns is a step toward preventing them from harming your relationships. If you notice yourself falling into one of these behaviors, you can pause and try a different approach.

---

## The Cycle of Resentment

Resentment is anger that has been stored away instead of dealt with. A woman might say to herself, "I will not fight about it," but inside, she is still upset. Over time, this hidden anger piles up. Each new slight or disagreement is added to the old ones. Eventually, a small issue can trigger a huge blow-up because all that stored anger comes spilling out.

Resentment can feel like a weight on a relationship. It colors the way you see the other person. Even if they do something nice, you might remain suspicious of their motives. You might keep a mental list of every wrong they have done. This attitude can block the possibility of finding common ground or rebuilding trust.

Letting go of resentment does not mean ignoring problems. Instead, it means finding a way to talk about them and seek solutions before they turn into a mountain of anger. If you find yourself feeling tense or bitter whenever you think about a certain person, that could be a sign of hidden resentment.

## Emotional Distance and Loss of Closeness

When anger regularly appears in a relationship, people often put up walls to protect themselves from hurt. This might mean sharing less about their day, not showing affection, or avoiding deep conversations. They might think, "It is easier to keep things shallow than to risk another fight."

Over time, these walls can become bigger. The emotional distance grows. A once-close bond might start to feel like two strangers living under the same roof or talking on the phone only out of obligation. This is a sad outcome for many women who want loving, supportive relationships. Recognizing that anger is driving a wedge between you and someone else is a key step in deciding to do something about it.

---

## Communication Breakdowns

Good communication is often the first thing to suffer when anger rises. People might talk in raised voices, interrupt each other, or toss out accusations without listening. In some cases, one person might speak in a mocking tone or roll their eyes, which makes the other person more upset. This back-and-forth can become a loop: anger leads to hurtful comments, which lead to more anger, and so on.

Once communication breaks down, it becomes harder to solve problems. Even if there is a genuine solution or compromise, anger can blind people to it. It can also block empathy—the ability to understand the other person's point of view. Without empathy, each person might only focus on winning the argument rather than understanding or fixing the problem.

---

## How Anger Influences Trust

Trust is the feeling that someone has your best interests at heart. It is also about believing that a person will not harm you. When anger is common in a relationship, trust can fade. You might start to think the other person wants to hurt you or does not care about your feelings. Or they might think the same about you. Even if neither of you truly wants to cause harm, constant anger creates that impression.

For example, if your partner sees you lose your temper for the tenth time in a month, they might worry that you do not respect them. If your friend sees you lash out at someone else, they might fear you will do the same to them. Trust is hard to rebuild once it is broken. Anger does not always destroy trust right away, but repeated episodes of uncontrolled anger can crack the foundation of any relationship.

---

## Unfair Expectations

Sometimes anger arises from unrealistic expectations we put on others. For instance, you might expect your partner to always sense when you are upset and fix the problem. Or you might feel that your friend should always agree with you. When reality does not match these expectations, you might get angry and accuse them of not caring enough.

In truth, everyone has limits and cannot meet all your needs. This does not mean you must accept poor treatment. But it does mean that placing high demands on a relationship can set you up for disappointment. Recognizing that others are human, with their own feelings and struggles, can help lower the chance of angry conflicts over minor issues.

---

## Hidden Triggers in Relationships

A woman might carry triggers from her past that come up in present relationships. Maybe she was hurt by a former partner who lied, so now she becomes angry at the slightest sign of dishonesty, even if her current partner did not lie. Or perhaps she had a parent who was very critical, so now any small critique from a friend feels like a huge attack.

These hidden triggers can cause confusion for both parties. The other person might have no idea why you are reacting with such anger. Meanwhile, you might not realize that old wounds are fueling your strong response. Being aware of these triggers can help you and the people in your life work around them or talk through them rather than fight about them.

## Effects on Group Settings

Sometimes anger does not just affect one-on-one relationships but also group dynamics. For instance, in a group of friends, if one person is often angry, the rest might start avoiding them. In a family gathering, an angry outburst can ruin the atmosphere for everyone. At work, a single person's anger can lower morale among an entire team.

People may feel they have to tiptoe around you to keep the peace. This can lead to tension and resentment. They might not share important information or invite you to certain events. This exclusion can make you feel even more upset or alone, creating a cycle of isolation fueled by anger.

## Recognizing When a Relationship Is Unhealthy

Anger can be a sign that a relationship has deeper issues. If someone is treating you poorly or harming you in any way, it is normal to feel angry. However, if you find yourself constantly blaming them for your anger without looking at your own actions, it might be worth taking a step back and asking: "Is this relationship truly supportive?" or "Am I contributing to the negativity?"

In some cases, anger becomes a tool for controlling or manipulating the other person. If you notice that you or someone else is using anger to scare, shame, or threaten, that is not a healthy dynamic. It might be best to seek professional help or set strong limits to protect your well-being.

## Preventing Angry Outbursts

Preventing anger from exploding in relationships requires awareness and practice. Some tips include:

1. **Pause Before Reacting**: If you feel a rush of anger, try to take a moment before you speak. You could step out of the room, count to ten, or focus on your breath for a minute.
2. **Use "I" Statements**: Say, "I feel upset when you do this," instead of "You make me mad." This can reduce the blame and help keep the other person from getting too defensive.
3. **Seek Clarity**: Ask questions to make sure you understand the other person's actions or words. Sometimes anger comes from misunderstandings.
4. **Agree to Disagree**: In relationships, you will not always see eye to eye. Knowing this can help you let go of the idea that someone must be right or wrong every time.

These strategies can help keep anger from boiling over. They do not fix every problem overnight, but they can reduce the damage anger might cause in the heat of the moment.

---

## Repairing Damage

If anger has already harmed a relationship, you may need to take steps to mend it. This could mean offering a sincere apology. It might also involve taking responsibility for your actions, such as admitting that you lashed out and agreeing to seek help or use better coping methods.

Sometimes, the other person might need time to heal. They might want to see a real change in your behavior before they trust you fully again. Patience is key. As you make progress in handling your anger, they can see the difference in how you behave. Over time, they may feel safe opening up to you again.

---

## Building Healthy Boundaries

Anger can flare when boundaries are unclear. For example, if a friend calls you at all hours to talk about their problems, you might become annoyed. Instead of snapping at them one day, it is better to set a boundary: tell them that you need rest during certain hours or that you cannot always talk about their concerns. By setting limits, you avoid the buildup of resentment.

Boundaries are also important if you are the one who gets angry often. Let others know when you need personal time to calm down. For instance, you can say, "I feel upset right now. I need ten minutes to clear my head before we continue." This small step can prevent arguments from exploding.

---

## Seeing Anger as a Signal, Not a Weapon

Anger can be a signal that something is wrong. It might show you that your needs are not being met, or that someone is crossing a line. But if you treat anger like a weapon, it can tear people apart. Using anger to frighten or punish others damages trust and pushes away the connection you might actually crave.

When you see anger as a signal, you can ask yourself: "What is this anger telling me about my needs, fears, or disappointments?" and "How can I share that information without attacking the other person?" This approach can shift the way you see conflict. Instead of seeing it as a battle to win, you can see it as a chance to talk openly and reach a better understanding.

---

## Moving Toward Better Relationships

While anger can harm relationships, it does not have to destroy them. By recognizing how anger affects the way you talk to and treat others, you can take steps to manage it. Healthy communication, fairness, and patience can help heal damaged bonds. You might need outside help from a counselor or mediator if the anger is deeply rooted or if trust has been badly broken.

Remember that relationships are built on mutual respect and support. If anger is allowed to take center stage, it reduces both respect and support on both sides. Taking responsibility for your own anger can inspire others to do the same. Over time, you can create a more caring environment where people feel safe being honest without fear of a hostile reaction.

# Chapter 5: Safe Ways to Express Anger

Anger itself is not bad. It can tell you that something matters to you or that someone has crossed a line you are not comfortable with. The problem is that many of us lack skills to release anger without harming ourselves or others. In this chapter, we will look at ways to let yourself feel and express anger in a manner that does not lead to regret or lasting damage. These methods can help you stay respectful toward others and yourself while still acknowledging your true feelings.

---

## Understanding the Need for Safe Outlets

Keeping anger bottled up can lead to bursts later on. Many women feel they must stay calm in all situations or risk being labeled as "difficult." As a result, they might bury anger, only to have it explode in an unrelated situation. Safe outlets let you handle anger bit by bit. If you can find a controlled way to let out steam, you are less likely to lash out at people close to you.

A "safe outlet" might be an activity, a setting, or a practice that allows you to recognize your anger, feel it, and release some of its intensity. This can involve physical movement, vocal expression, or calm reflection. Each person has to find what works best for them. One person might like writing down her thoughts, while another might prefer talking with a trusted friend.

---

## Physical Activities

For some women, anger is felt most strongly in the body. You might notice tense muscles, a racing heart, or a hot feeling in your face. Physical activities can help release that energy in a controlled way. Here are a few ideas:

1. **Walking or Jogging**
   Taking a brisk walk or easy jog can help burn off the tension that builds with anger. Pay attention to your surroundings as you move. Notice the sights and sounds. This might help slow your racing thoughts. You do not

have to walk or jog for a very long time; even ten minutes can make a difference. The key is to let your body use the energy that anger stirs up.
2. **Punching a Pillow**
This might sound silly, but hitting a pillow (or another soft, safe object) can let you release energy without harming yourself or anything else. Some women find it helpful to let out a yell into the pillow. This private moment can give you a quick release of stored anger.
3. **Dancing or Stretching**
Turning on music and moving to it can let you express anger through motion. You might choose loud, energetic music that matches your mood. Or you might prefer slower music if you want to calm down. Stretching can also help ease tight muscles, reminding your body that it is safe to relax.
4. **Household Chores**
Activities like scrubbing the floor or cleaning the windows can help you burn energy while also doing something productive. This might serve as a double benefit: you get a cleaner space and you feel more at ease. Just be sure not to rush or slam things around in a harmful way.

Physical outlets can be a quick fix, giving your body something to do with the anger. Afterward, you may feel clearer. It is often a good idea to follow these activities with a calmer practice, like deep breathing or resting, so your body can shift fully out of the angry state.

---

## Writing or Drawing

Some people find it easier to handle anger by putting thoughts on paper:

1. **Writing Letters You Do Not Send**
You can write a letter to the person or situation that upset you. Pour out everything you feel. Do not hold back. Once you are done, you can tear up the letter, throw it away, or keep it in a private place. The goal is not to send it but to let your feelings flow out safely.
2. **Private Journals**
Keep a journal to record angry moments. Write down what happened, how you felt, and what you wish you could say or do. Over time, you

might notice patterns in your anger triggers. You can also use the journal to list ideas for solving or avoiding those triggers in the future.

3. **Art or Coloring**
   Drawing, painting, or coloring can give your anger a form that does not involve words. You might draw shapes or scribbles that represent your mood. You can also color in patterns or mandalas (if you enjoy that kind of art). By focusing on lines and colors, you might find your mind calming and your anger shifting into a more relaxed state.

Writing and drawing serve as safe outlets because they let you express yourself without involving another person directly. You do not have to worry about saying the "wrong" thing. You can be as open as you want. This can be freeing if you often hold back your anger in daily life.

---

## Vocal Expression

Anger often feels like it is caught in your throat. You might sense a need to shout or say something you have been holding back. Letting words or sounds out in a careful way can help. Below are some suggestions:

1. **Screaming in a Private Space**
   You could step into a garage, a car (with windows up), or a space away from others, then let out a loud yell. This can feel like releasing a valve that has too much pressure. Make sure you choose a place where you will not scare others or draw unwanted attention.
2. **Reading or Reciting Something Aloud**
   If screaming feels too intense, you might recite a poem, a prayer, or even a piece of writing that captures your feelings. Speaking with emotion can help you move some of the anger out of your body. You are giving your anger a voice without directing it at a specific person.
3. **Talking to a Trusted Friend**
   Sometimes you just need someone to hear you out. Choose a friend who is good at listening and who will not judge you for venting. You might start by saying, "I need to let some anger out. Could you listen for a few minutes?" This friend does not have to fix the situation. They just need to offer understanding.

Vocal expression can bring quick relief, but it is important to respect those around you. Make sure you are not yelling at someone who is not ready to hear it or using harmful language. Aim for ways that let you shout or speak without leaving scars on another person.

## Practice Calming the Body Afterward

Once you have expressed anger, do not forget to soothe your body and mind. Otherwise, you might stay on edge. Here are a few gentle ideas:

1. **Deep Breathing**
   Take a slow breath in through the nose for a count of four, hold for a moment, then let the breath out through the mouth for a count of four. Repeat several times. Feel your shoulders drop and your jaw relax.
2. **Progressive Muscle Relaxation**
   Tense each major muscle group in your body for a few seconds, then relax. Start with your feet, then move up to your calves, thighs, and so on. This helps clear out lingering tension.
3. **Warm Bath or Shower**
   Water can be soothing. A bath or shower gives you private time to let the heat relax your muscles. If you like scents, a mild soap or lotion can help shift your mood.
4. **Quiet Time**
   Sit in a calm spot, close your eyes, and let your mind rest. If thoughts pop up, try not to attach to them. Just notice them and let them go. Even five minutes of quiet can help your body settle.

Soothing your body reminds your system that the danger has passed. It helps you come down from the adrenaline rush anger can bring. This step is important for your health and helps you feel in control again.

## Healthy Outlets in Public

Anger sometimes flares in public places—on the job, at a store, or at a family event. You might not have the privacy to scream or punch a pillow. You still need ways to let off steam safely. Consider these tips:

1. **Focus on Your Breathing**
   You can do this without anyone noticing. Breathe slowly, trying to make your exhale longer than your inhale. This can calm your racing heartbeat and keep you from saying something you might regret.
2. **Use Grounding Methods**
   Look around and note five things you see. Then note four things you can hear, three things you can touch, two things you can smell, and one thing you can taste (if possible). This simple mental exercise shifts your focus from anger to the world around you, reducing the intensity of your feelings.
3. **Step Away**
   If a conversation is making you furious, politely excuse yourself. Say something like, "I need a moment," and find a more private corner or restroom. Take a short walk or splash water on your face. This time-out can prevent a bigger blow-up.
4. **Write in Your Phone's Notes**
   If you cannot speak freely, you can open the notes app on your phone and type what you are feeling. Imagine you are texting a friend, but do not send it. This quick release can help you stay composed on the outside.

These methods do not make your anger vanish, but they prevent you from creating a scene or hurting someone in the heat of the moment. After you have calmed down, you can decide if you need a more private form of expression later.

---

## Anger and Creative Expression

Art, music, and other creative hobbies can be powerful ways to handle anger. For instance, if you play an instrument, you might pour your energy into playing it more forcefully (but safely). If you like sculpting, you might shape clay in a way that reflects your upset emotions. If you enjoy spoken word, you might record voice notes to capture your thoughts.

There is no single right method here. The idea is to channel anger into something that can be created rather than destroyed. When you finish, you might feel proud that you turned a tense feeling into something meaningful. This can lessen guilt or shame you might feel about being angry. It can also help you see anger as a spark for action, rather than a shameful emotion that must be hidden.

## The Difference Between Safe Expression and Harmful Actions

Expressing anger safely means not causing harm to yourself, others, or property. It also means not relying on destructive habits to cope, such as substance abuse or self-harm. Here are some points that separate healthy outlets from harmful actions:

- **Healthy Outlets**: Venting to a friend, physical exercise, writing in a journal, mindful breathing, or doing something creative.
- **Harmful Actions**: Yelling at or insulting someone, throwing objects in anger, hurting yourself, turning to alcohol or drugs for relief, or threatening others.

Sometimes, people think that if they do not lash out, they are not truly expressing anger. But you can feel and release anger without shouting or slamming doors. Safe expression is about honesty paired with respect—for yourself, others, and your environment.

## Setting Boundaries on Your Expression

Even safe forms of expression can cross a line if they go on too long or happen at the wrong place and time. It is wise to set certain limits for yourself:

1. **Time Limits**
   If you are journaling your anger, you might set a 15-minute timer. Give yourself that period to write freely. After that, make a choice to pause. This stops you from cycling through the same angry thoughts for hours.
2. **Respect for Shared Spaces**
   If you live with others, be mindful of where you express your anger. Screaming late at night could wake them. Physical outlets like hitting a pillow should happen in a place where you will not break items or make others feel unsafe.

3. **Honesty with Others**
   If you plan to vent to a friend, ask for their permission first. Some people might be dealing with their own stresses and cannot handle another person's anger at that moment. Show you respect their boundaries too.

By setting these limits, you protect yourself and those around you from negative fallout. You also build a positive habit of handling anger in a measured way.

---

## When Safe Expression Is Not Enough

Sometimes, anger runs too deep for simple outlets to manage. You might notice that even after journaling or punching a pillow, you are still boiling inside. This can happen if your anger is tied to bigger life issues—like ongoing unfair treatment, painful memories, or repeated hurts in a relationship. In these cases, you might need more structured help. This could include:

- **Therapy or Counseling**: A professional can help you unpack deep-seated anger and teach you long-term coping methods.
- **Support Groups**: Meeting others who share similar struggles can ease the sense of isolation. Hearing their experiences may also offer new ideas for handling anger.
- **Changes in Your Environment**: If you are in an unfair job setting or a harsh home environment, you might need to make broader changes. Safe expression can help you cope day to day, but real relief might come from improving the situation itself.

Recognizing when personal efforts are not enough is a sign of strength, not weakness. It shows you value your well-being and are ready to seek the right kind of help.

---

## Handling Anger in Conversations

When you are angry at a specific person, you may need to talk to them rather than let your anger out alone. Here are some tips to keep it as safe and respectful as possible:

1. **Use Calm Language**
   Instead of saying, "You never listen to me!" say, "I feel upset because I do not think my thoughts are being heard." This phrasing focuses on your feelings rather than blaming them.
2. **Stick to the Issue**
   Do not bring up past mistakes just to make the other person feel bad. Focus on the current matter. If you need to address past events, talk about them one at a time instead of piling them all on at once.
3. **Listen Actively**
   After you speak, let the other person respond. Keep yourself from interrupting or rolling your eyes. Even if you disagree, show you are hearing them. This will encourage them to hear you as well.
4. **Agree to Take Breaks**
   If things get too heated, agree to pause and come back to the discussion later. Both of you might need time to cool down and collect your thoughts.

Safe expression in a conversation means sharing your anger without crossing into personal attacks. It can be uncomfortable, but clear communication can often lead to mutual understanding.

---

# Tips for Daily Life

Anger can pop up in daily life—while driving, shopping, or doing chores. Having short, simple tools ready can help you avoid outbursts:

- **Count to Ten**: A classic tip, but it works. Focus on counting slowly. This short distraction can keep you from acting on impulse.
- **Name the Feeling**: Silently say to yourself, "I am angry," or "I am annoyed." Just naming it can help you gain some control.
- **Move Your Body**: Do a quick set of knee bends, shoulder rolls, or neck stretches. These small actions can release tension fast.
- **Repeat a Soothing Phrase**: It might be, "I can handle this," or "This will pass." Say it a few times in your mind to ground yourself.

These mini-strategies are not a full solution. They simply help you pause so you can choose a better response when anger tries to take over.

## The Value of Practice

Expressing anger safely is not always natural. You might have grown up seeing anger expressed in loud or damaging ways, or you might have been taught never to show anger at all. Either way, learning a new approach takes time. You might not get it right every time. You may still slip and yell. That is okay. The key is to keep practicing.

Over time, safe expression becomes easier. You learn to catch anger early, before it explodes. You also learn that letting anger out in a healthy way does not make you a bad person. In fact, it can improve your sense of self-control and reduce the guilt you might feel after an outburst.

---

## Combining Methods

You do not have to pick just one method. Many women find it helps to mix different outlets. For example, you might choose to go for a short run to burn off some energy, then come home and write a letter in your journal. Or you might call a friend to vent, then use deep breathing to settle your body. Experiment with various approaches until you find a few that fit your lifestyle and comfort level.

---

## Looking Ahead

Safe expression of anger is a big step in healing the stress anger can bring. It does not solve every conflict, but it helps you approach problems with a calmer mind. In the next chapter, we will talk about building self-awareness, which goes hand in hand with safe expression. When you know yourself—your triggers, your physical cues, your thought patterns—you can respond to anger more wisely.

Anger is powerful, but it does not have to be destructive. By finding outlets that keep you and others safe, you can allow anger to move through you instead of letting it build up or burst out in harmful ways. Whether you choose a physical approach, a creative outlet, or a quiet conversation, the aim is the same: to honor your feelings in a balanced manner.

# Chapter 6: Building Self-Awareness

Knowing yourself is a key part of managing anger. Self-awareness means understanding your own patterns—what triggers you, what physical signals show up when you start getting mad, and what thoughts might make you more upset. The more you understand about your inner world, the better you can handle anger before it explodes. In this chapter, we will look at why self-awareness matters and how to develop it in everyday life.

---

## Why Self-Awareness Is Important

When a person lacks self-awareness, anger can catch them off guard. They might say, "I just exploded out of nowhere!" But anger rarely appears without warning. Often, there are small signs in the body or mind. Self-awareness helps you see those signs early.

Being aware of your triggers and bodily changes can help you pause and choose a safe outlet. You might notice your shoulders tense or your breathing becomes shallow. Or you might feel a slight headache creeping in. These are warnings your body sends. If you are in tune with them, you can act before you reach a breaking point. Self-awareness also helps you learn from mistakes. If you reflect on an outburst and notice what led to it, you can address that factor next time.

---

## Tracking Your Anger Patterns

One practical way to build self-awareness is to keep track of your anger in a simple log or journal. It does not have to be fancy. You can note details like:

- **Date and Time**: When did you feel angry?
- **Situation**: What was happening? Who was there?
- **Body Clues**: What physical signs did you notice? Headache, tight jaw, sweating?
- **Thoughts**: What were you telling yourself?
- **Action**: How did you respond? Yell, walk away, or something else?

- **Aftermath**: How did you feel later? Did it solve the problem, or did it lead to regret?

Reviewing your notes each week can reveal patterns. Maybe you get angry most when you are hungry or tired. Maybe certain people or tasks annoy you more than others. You might also notice the same thought popping up, like "No one respects me." Recognizing these patterns is the first step to addressing them.

---

## Mindful Observation

Mindfulness is about paying attention to the present moment without judging it. You can use mindfulness to observe your body, thoughts, and feelings as they happen. This does not mean you push anger away. Instead, you watch it arise and learn about it in a calm manner. Below are some ways to practice mindful observation:

1. **Body Scan**
   Sit quietly and focus on one area of your body at a time. Start with your toes and move up slowly, noticing any tension. Do this daily, even when you are not angry. You will get better at spotting tight muscles or changes in your heartbeat as soon as they happen.
2. **Thought Watching**
   Imagine your thoughts as clouds passing across the sky. When a thought appears—like "This is so unfair"—just notice it. Then imagine it drifting away. Try not to jump in and argue with the thought. This trains you to see your thinking patterns without getting stuck in them.
3. **Emotion Labeling**
   When an emotion arises, name it: "I feel angry," or "I feel frustrated." By labeling it, you gain a bit of distance from the emotion. This can stop you from acting on it right away. You might say, "Okay, anger is here," instead of letting anger take complete control.

Mindful observation can feel strange at first. You might worry that you are not doing it right. That is normal. The key is to practice a little each day. Over time, you will become more attuned to what your mind and body are doing, which helps you spot anger before it grows too large.

## Learning Your Triggers

A trigger is something that sparks anger. It can be a person's tone of voice, a certain topic, or even something as small as a messy room. Different people have different triggers. Knowing yours is vital for staying calm. Here are some steps to identify triggers:

1. **Reflect on Past Incidents**
   Think about the last few times you got mad. Ask: "What set me off? Was there a word, action, or event that pushed me over the edge?" Write down any repeats you see.
2. **Notice Physical Spaces**
   Sometimes the environment can be a trigger. For example, you might feel more on edge in a cluttered room or in heavy traffic. Stressful surroundings can increase the chance of an outburst.
3. **Reflect on Past Hurts**
   Old wounds can turn into triggers. If you were often ignored as a child, you might get especially angry when someone cuts you off mid-sentence. By recognizing this link, you can respond with more awareness next time.
4. **Look for Patterns in Your Mood**
   Sometimes, you are more prone to anger if you are already upset or worried. A small trigger can then set off a big reaction. Notice if your mood or stress level is playing a role.

Once you know your triggers, you can plan how to handle them. For instance, if traffic is a big problem, you might leave earlier to avoid the worst congestion or bring along calming music. If a certain discussion topic with a friend triggers you, you might set boundaries about when or how to talk about it.

---

## Understanding Your Thoughts

Thoughts play a large role in anger. What you tell yourself in the heat of a moment can fuel your reaction. Here are some common thought patterns that might increase anger:

- **All-or-Nothing Thinking**: Believing that if one thing goes wrong, everything is ruined. For instance, "They forgot my birthday, so they must not care about me at all."

- **Labeling**: Putting harsh labels on people or situations, such as "That person is a total fool," or "I am such a failure."
- **Mind Reading**: Assuming you know what others are thinking, often in a negative way, like "They are only saying that to make me look bad."
- **Fortune Telling**: Predicting the worst outcome without real proof: "I just know this meeting will be a disaster."

When you notice these patterns, pause and ask: "Is this thought completely true? Do I have real evidence?" Often, these thoughts stretch the truth, making your anger flare. By challenging them, you can reduce anger's grip.

---

## Checking Your Body's Signals

Your body might give you clues that anger is building:

- **Tight Chest**: You may find it hard to breathe deeply.
- **Clenched Jaw**: Your teeth might grind or your jaw might ache.
- **Pounding Heart**: Your pulse might speed up.
- **Sweaty Palms**: You might notice moisture forming in your hands.
- **Stomach Problems**: You might feel a knot in your belly.

These signals often come before you explode. If you can catch them early, you can decide to step away or use a calming method. This helps you respond instead of just reacting on autopilot.

---

## Emotional Awareness

Anger can hide other emotions underneath—sadness, fear, shame. Self-awareness means identifying these hidden feelings. Here is how you can explore that:

1. **Ask "What Else Am I Feeling?"**
   When anger surfaces, pause and see if any other feeling is there. Are you sad because someone hurt your feelings? Are you afraid of losing control in a situation?

2. **Rate Your Anger**
   On a scale of 1 to 10, how angry are you? Then, rate any other emotion you sense. You might find that sadness is at an 8, while anger is at a 6. This can help you understand which emotion is bigger, so you can address it properly.
3. **Write Down Words That Come to Mind**
   If naming feelings is hard, quickly jot down words or short phrases. It might look like "betrayed, lonely, powerless." Seeing these words can help you realize your anger might be covering pain or vulnerability.

Understanding these deeper emotions does not make anger invalid. It simply helps you see the full picture. You can then decide if you need comfort, reassurance, or a conversation rather than an angry outburst.

---

## Self-Talk for Self-Awareness

Self-talk is the inner conversation you have with yourself. Shifting it in a positive direction can boost self-awareness. For example:

- **Change "I'm losing it!" to "I feel very upset, but I can manage."**
  This small tweak reminds you that you have options.
- **Change "They are doing this on purpose!" to "I might be reading into their actions. Let me check the facts."**
  This keeps you from jumping to conclusions.
- **Change "I have no control!" to "I can step away or try a different approach."**
  This gives you a sense of choice.

Being aware of your self-talk can prevent anger from spiraling. It also helps you feel less helpless, because you remind yourself that you can respond thoughtfully.

---

## Meditation and Quiet Reflection

Some women find that setting aside time for silent reflection helps them notice early signs of anger. This does not have to be long or complicated. Even five minutes each morning can help:

1. **Sit Comfortably**
   Choose a position where you can stay still without pain.
2. **Focus on Your Breath**
   Inhale through your nose, exhale through your mouth. Notice the rise and fall of your chest.
3. **Let Thoughts Pass**
   If you catch yourself thinking, gently bring your focus back to breathing.
4. **End with a Check-In**
   When you finish, ask yourself, "How do I feel right now?" "Is there any tension in my body?" This daily habit can make you more tuned in to changes in your mood.

Over time, this practice can sharpen your skill at spotting anger early. You will develop a habit of observing yourself calmly, which can help you in tense moments.

---

## Seeking Feedback from Others

Sometimes it is hard to see our own patterns. Trusted friends or family members might notice when you start to get upset before you do. If you feel open to it, you can ask them to point out when they see warning signs. For example, "If you notice I am clenching my fists or raising my voice, could you let me know?"

However, be sure to choose someone who is caring and respectful. It should be someone who will bring it up in a calm way, not to shame you, but to help you stay aware. This kind of external feedback can shine a light on blind spots you might have.

---

## Creating a Personal Anger Scale

A personal anger scale can help you measure how close you are to losing control. You might label levels from 1 to 10:

- **1**: Calm or only slightly annoyed.
- **3**: You feel irritated, but you can still speak politely.
- **5**: You notice tension in your body, your tone might get sharper.

- **7**: Your voice is loud, you might feel the urge to slam things.
- **9**: You are on the edge of a full-outburst.
- **10**: You have lost control and are reacting in a harmful way.

By checking in with yourself and assigning a number, you can gauge when you need to use a safe outlet. If you notice you are at a 6, you might decide to take a break from the conversation before you climb to an 8 or 9.

---

## Avoiding Shame

Some women feel shame just for having anger. They might have grown up with the belief that a "good girl" never gets mad. If this is the case for you, it is important to separate the fact of being angry from feeling shame about it. Anger is a normal emotion. It points to something you care about. Building self-awareness does not mean trying to get rid of anger. It means noticing it and guiding it in a healthy way.

If you catch yourself thinking, "I'm horrible for being angry," challenge that. Replace it with, "I am angry because I care about something. I can handle this feeling." Self-awareness includes kindness toward yourself.

---

## Handling Surprises

Life is full of surprises that can spark anger. A last-minute work request, a flat tire, or a rude comment from a stranger can all throw you off. Self-awareness prepares you for the unexpected. You might not know what will happen, but you do know how your body and mind respond to stress. With this knowledge, you can apply your coping skills on the spot.

For example, if you feel your heart pounding when you read a harsh email, you can pause and breathe before typing a reply. You might think, "I'm climbing up my anger scale right now. I need to do something before I respond." This mental pause could save you from sending a message you regret.

---

## Small Steps Every Day

Self-awareness grows with practice. Think of small ways to learn about yourself each day:

- **Take a Midday Check-In**: Around lunchtime, ask yourself, "How am I feeling?" If you sense tension, do a quick relaxation exercise.
- **End-of-Day Reflection**: Before bed, think about any moments you felt frustrated or angry. Write a sentence or two about what happened.
- **Use Triggers as Teachers**: Each time you notice a trigger, thank yourself for spotting it. Remind yourself this is progress in understanding your anger.

These small habits keep you in touch with your inner state. You do not have to wait until anger explodes to pay attention.

---

## Combining Self-Awareness with Action

Self-awareness is not just about noticing anger; it is about deciding what to do with it. Once you see that you are at a 6 on your anger scale, you can choose a safe outlet from Chapter 5. Or if you notice your thoughts turning harsh, you can challenge them or step away. This link between awareness and action is what really makes the difference in anger control.

If you fail to act on what you notice, you may still end up feeling out of control. That is why building a toolbox of calming methods is so crucial. Self-awareness alerts you. Calming methods help you respond.

---

## The Growth of Self-Understanding

Over time, self-awareness leads to a deeper understanding of who you are. You might discover that your anger mostly arises from feeling dismissed. Or maybe you find that you get mad when you are worried about failing. These insights do not fix everything at once, but they guide you to the root of the problem.

For example, if you learn that you hate feeling dismissed, you can work on being more assertive about your ideas. If you see that fear of failure sparks anger, you can address that fear directly—perhaps by talking with a mentor or practicing positive self-talk. Self-awareness shines a light on the issues that fuel anger, letting you tackle them head-on.

---

## Moving Forward

As you grow more self-aware, you will likely see changes in how you handle anger. You might catch yourself before you yell. You might take a walk instead of getting into a heated argument. You might talk openly about your triggers with people you trust. All these steps show that self-awareness is paying off.

In the chapters ahead, we will look at more strategies for communication and conflict resolution. These skills, combined with self-awareness, will help you keep anger from ruling your life. You can still feel anger—it is a natural emotion—but you will have the knowledge and tools to manage it wisely.

Building self-awareness takes patience, but it lays a solid foundation for healthier living. Each time you notice an anger trigger or a bodily signal, you are moving toward a place of choice rather than blind reaction. This shift brings more calm and confidence, allowing you to connect with others in a way that respects both your feelings and theirs.

# Chapter 7: Learning Better Communication

Communication has a big impact on how anger unfolds. Sometimes, misunderstandings spark anger because both sides are talking without really listening. Other times, one person might hold back words until anger builds. In either case, learning how to speak and listen more clearly can reduce anger levels and help you express needs in a healthier way. In this chapter, we will talk about methods to improve communication so that anger does not take over your conversations.

## Why Good Communication Matters

When you share information clearly, others have a better chance of understanding what you want or need. When they do the same, you feel included and heard. Anger often appears when you think someone is ignoring your wishes or brushing off your concerns. Good communication can lower this risk by letting you and the other person know exactly what is going on, even if you do not agree. It creates a sense of respect and shows that both sides matter.

Also, good communication is not just about speaking. It includes active listening, facial expressions, body posture, tone of voice, and more. If these parts of communication go wrong, you might feel attacked or judged, and anger can rise. By getting better at these skills, you can make sure your messages come across in ways that keep anger in check.

## Speaking Clearly and Calmly

When anger flares up, it is tempting to shout or throw out harsh words. But doing so usually pushes the other person away and can lead to bigger fights. Speaking clearly and calmly is a way to share your honest feelings without hurting the person in front of you. Below are some tips:

1. **Use Simple Words**
   Stick to basic language instead of long or harsh terms. Saying, "I am upset because I feel left out" is clearer than saying, "You are completely

thoughtless for ignoring me." By keeping words simple, you keep the conversation focused on the problem instead of fueling it with insults.
2. **Stay on One Issue**
If you bring up multiple complaints at once, the other person might feel overwhelmed or attacked. If you are upset that your friend was late, discuss that issue alone. Avoid dragging in old events or unrelated topics. Keeping focus on one problem makes it easier to solve that problem.
3. **Pick an Appropriate Time and Place**
It is not helpful to have a serious talk in the middle of a noisy event or when the other person is rushed. Find a moment and setting where both of you can concentrate. If possible, pick a private place without distractions, so you both feel safe sharing your thoughts.
4. **Stay Aware of Your Tone**
A calm tone shows you are open to finding a fair solution. A loud or sarcastic tone can suggest you have already judged the other person. When you hear your voice rising, pause and try to speak at a lower volume. This quick shift can help keep the conversation from turning into a fight.

---

## The Value of "I" Statements

One of the most common tips in communication is to use "I" statements instead of "you" statements. This simple change can have a big effect. An "I" statement tells the other person how you feel, what you are experiencing, and what you hope for. A "you" statement often sounds like blame or accusation. Here are some examples:

- **"You" Statement**: "You always ignore what I say. You never pay attention!"
- **"I" Statement**: "I feel hurt when I am talking and it seems like I am not being heard."

Notice how the "I" statement does not point a finger. It focuses on your feelings and invites the other person to understand your view. That makes it easier for them to respond without becoming defensive.

A basic formula for "I" statements is:

1. "I feel _ _ _ _" (name the emotion you are experiencing)

2. "When _____ happens" (describe the specific behavior or situation)
3. "Because _____" (explain why this situation affects you)
4. "I would like _____" (state what you want or need in the future)

For instance: "I feel frustrated when my opinions are dismissed because it makes me think I am not respected. I would like us to talk about everyone's views before deciding."

---

## Active Listening

Communication is not just about speaking; it is about hearing the other side too. Active listening means you fully pay attention to what the speaker is saying, instead of planning your own reply or judging their words. Some methods for active listening include:

1. **Maintain Eye Contact**
   Look at the person speaking (if it feels comfortable and appropriate). This shows you are focused on them. Try not to glance at your phone or around the room.
2. **Use Open Body Language**
   Folded arms or a rigid posture can give the impression that you are closed off. Aim to face them directly, perhaps with relaxed shoulders, to show openness.
3. **Nod or Give Brief Verbal Feedback**
   Saying "I see," or "Yes, I understand," tells the speaker you are following along. Nodding also helps show you are tracking their words.
4. **Restate What You Heard**
   When the person finishes, summarize what they said in your own words. For example: "So you are saying you felt ignored because I was on my phone during our conversation, right?" This step helps them know you really listened. It also gives them a chance to correct you if you misunderstood.
5. **Ask Clarifying Questions**
   If something is unclear, ask gently: "Can you explain a bit more about how that made you feel?" This shows you care about fully grasping their perspective.

When you practice active listening, you are less likely to respond in anger. You can actually hear what the other person is saying, which might calm some of your own negative assumptions. This can lead to more helpful discussions, rather than back-and-forth arguments.

---

## Avoiding Hurtful Language

Words carry power. In moments of anger, it is easy to use hurtful remarks or names. While these may vent your frustration for a second, they can leave scars that linger. Examples of hurtful language include:

- Name-calling ("You are so stupid!")
- Generalizations ("You never do anything right!")
- Comparisons ("Why can't you be like my friend's husband?")
- Criticizing someone's character instead of their behavior ("You are a lazy person," vs. "I wish you would help with household tasks more often.")

Instead, aim your words at the behavior or situation, not at the person. For example, "It bothers me when dishes pile up" is less hurtful than "You are useless around the house." This approach keeps the focus on the real problem and avoids deep personal attacks that can spark lasting anger.

---

## Nonverbal Signals

Body language can speak volumes, sometimes more strongly than words. Even if you speak calmly, your nonverbal signals might say something else. Anger can show up in rolling eyes, sighing loudly, or turning away. These signals can annoy or anger the person you are talking to. Here are ways to keep your nonverbal cues in check:

1. **Stay Mindful of Your Face**
   Facial expressions like frowning or glaring can send a strong message. Try to keep a neutral or concerned look, showing you are taking the matter seriously without being hostile.
2. **Watch Your Hands**
   Pointing a finger or making a fist can come across as threatening. If you

feel tense, you can fold your hands gently in your lap or let them rest on a table.
3. **Limit Aggressive Gestures**
Sudden movements, standing over someone while they are seated, or leaning in too close can make the other person feel uncomfortable. Keep a respectful distance unless you have a close personal relationship where you both feel okay being near each other.
4. **Use a Softer Tone**
Sometimes your voice can get sharper even if you are not yelling. If you notice yourself sounding sarcastic or cold, take a breath and try to speak in a more measured tone.

---

## Setting Boundaries for Communication

Communication can fail if there are no clear boundaries. Boundaries are rules or limits that keep conversations respectful. For example, you and a friend or partner might agree never to swear at each other, slam doors, or threaten to leave mid-discussion. Or you might both decide on a maximum time you will spend talking about a single issue before taking a break.

Some people find it helpful to have a "safe word" or phrase that signals, "I need to pause this talk right now." This can prevent a small disagreement from becoming a full-blown fight. You then come back to the issue once both sides are calmer.

These boundaries do not mean you are ignoring the problem. They mean you are setting up rules to stop the conversation from becoming harmful. Over time, these rules can turn into habits that keep your discussions more civil, even when the topics are tough.

---

## Being Assertive, Not Aggressive

Assertiveness means clearly stating your needs or opinions while also respecting the other person's rights and feelings. It differs from aggression, which often disregards someone else's feelings and can include threatening behavior. Here is how to practice assertiveness:

1. **Know Your Goal**
   Before you start talking, ask yourself: "What do I hope to achieve?" If your goal is to solve a scheduling conflict, keep the focus on that. Avoid turning the talk into a blame game.
2. **Express Feelings Firmly But Calmly**
   For example, "I feel upset because I think my work is not being appreciated," said with a steady tone, is assertive. Shouting, "You all ignore me and it's unfair!" is more aggressive and less likely to lead to a good resolution.
3. **Invite the Other Side to Respond**
   Assertiveness includes giving the other person a chance to speak. You can say, "How do you see this situation?" or "I want to hear your thoughts." This shows respect and keeps the conversation balanced.
4. **Stay Confident in Your Right to Speak**
   Part of assertiveness is believing you have the right to be heard. If you find yourself apologizing too much for having feelings, remind yourself that your feelings do matter. You can stay polite while still standing up for yourself.

Being assertive can take practice if you are used to either staying silent or blowing up in anger. Start with smaller situations and build from there. Over time, you might find that others respond better to an assertive tone than to a quiet or explosive one.

---

## Apologizing When Needed

Sometimes in an argument, you might say or do something unfair. Recognizing your own mistakes can go a long way toward healing anger on both sides. A good apology is clear and sincere. It might look like this:

- **Step 1**: Admit what you did. ("I snapped at you and called you a name.")
- **Step 2**: Express regret. ("I feel terrible about it.")
- **Step 3**: Offer to fix it if possible. ("If there is something I can do to make it up, please tell me.")

- **Step 4**: Share your plan to do better next time. ("From now on, I will take a short break before responding when I am upset.")

This type of apology does not try to shift blame. It also avoids excuses like "I was just tired." Instead, it admits fault and shows you value the relationship enough to make changes. Even if the other person is not ready to forgive right away, a sincere apology can lower the tension and open the door to better communication later.

## Working Through Differences

Communication does not always lead to agreement. Even when both sides speak and listen well, you might still disagree. This is normal. Good communication is not about forcing someone to see things your way. It is about understanding each other's positions. Sometimes, you can agree to disagree without letting anger destroy the relationship. Other times, you might find a compromise or solution that pleases everyone.

If you find yourselves stuck, you can say, "It seems we cannot agree on this right now. Let's set this aside and see if we can brainstorm more options later." This approach respects the other person's time and views, rather than keeping you in a dead-end talk.

## Staying Aware of Cultural or Personality Differences

Not everyone communicates in the same way. Some cultures value directness, while others see direct complaints as rude. Some people prefer to share everything on their mind, while others hold back until they feel truly comfortable. If you or the person you are speaking with comes from a different background or has a different personality style, misread signals can cause anger.

Try to be open and curious about how the other person prefers to communicate. Ask questions if you are unsure. For example, "Do you prefer talking about problems right away, or do you need time to think first?" This respectful curiosity can prevent anger that arises from clashing styles.

## Handling Interruptions

When you are talking, being interrupted can be frustrating. If this leads to anger, consider these points:

1. **Politely Point It Out**
   You can say, "I'd like to finish my thought, please." This is more effective than snapping, "Stop interrupting me!"
2. **Stay Calm**
   They might not realize they are interrupting. Keep your tone measured.
3. **Set a Rule**
   In some settings, you can set a ground rule: each person gets a certain amount of time to speak without interruption. This ensures everyone feels heard.

---

## Checking for Understanding

After a discussion, it helps to see if both sides understand the key points. You can do a quick recap:

- "So, you are saying you would prefer if I text you in advance before dropping by your house. And from my side, I would appreciate if you do not tease me about my schedule. Does that sound right to you?"

This simple habit can catch any miscommunication before it grows into anger. It also helps both sides remember what was decided, so they can stick to it in the future.

---

## Recognizing Stonewalling

Stonewalling is when someone shuts down and refuses to talk at all. They might leave the room, ignore the speaker, or just go silent. This often happens because the person feels too overwhelmed to respond. Stonewalling can increase anger, because the other side might feel ignored. If you notice stonewalling in yourself or someone else, you can say:

- "I need a short break. I am feeling overwhelmed. Can we return to this topic in 15 minutes?"

This approach admits that you need a pause instead of giving the other person the silent treatment. Scheduling a time to continue means you are not just running away, but rather gathering your composure so you can talk better.

---

## When to Seek Outside Help

If you try these communication tips and still find that anger rules your talks, it might be time to get help from a neutral third party. This could be a counselor, a mediator, or a trusted mentor. They can guide the discussion, help each side speak fairly, and offer tools you might not have tried. Sometimes, having a trained person in the room keeps both parties on track. This is not a sign of failure; it is a wise step to protect relationships and mental well-being.

---

## Steps for Ongoing Improvement

Improving communication is a process. You can do small things each day to build your skills:

- **Practice "I" statements in low-stakes settings**: Try them when chatting with a friend about simple topics before using them in tense situations.
- **Role-play with a friend**: If you have to talk about a difficult topic, you can practice how you will phrase things. Ask for feedback on your tone and body language.
- **Watch how calm speakers talk**: Notice people you admire who communicate calmly, even under stress. Observe their word choices, posture, and tone of voice. See if you can adopt some of these habits.
- **Reflect after each discussion**: If a talk goes well, think about what helped. If it goes poorly, think about what you could do differently next time.

These habits can slowly change the way you communicate, lowering anger for you and the people around you. As you learn to speak more kindly and listen more fully, your relationships may feel less tense. That shift can also reduce the frequency and intensity of angry outbursts.

## Tying It Together

Communication plays a major role in anger. When you say what you mean in a clear, respectful way, and when you listen deeply to what others say, you can address problems before they become explosive. No one is perfect, and every conversation will not be flawless. However, even small improvements in how you express yourself can make a big difference.

In the next chapter, we will look at specific ways to solve conflicts. You will learn methods to handle disagreements so they do not turn into drawn-out battles. Combined with better communication, these methods can help you handle anger triggers with greater ease, leading to healthier relationships at home, at work, and elsewhere.

# Chapter 8: Ways to Solve Conflicts

Conflicts are a normal part of life. People will always have disagreements, whether at home, at work, or with friends. The key is how you handle them. Anger often arises when conflicts get stuck in a pattern of blame or heated exchanges. This chapter will give you practical steps to address conflicts more effectively and minimize the harmful effects of anger on your relationships.

---

## Why Conflicts Arise

Before we explore solutions, let us look at why conflicts happen in the first place:

1. **Different Needs and Goals**
   Two people might want different things at the same time. For example, one family member wants a quiet evening while another wants to watch a loud movie. If they cannot agree on a compromise, conflict emerges.
2. **Poor Communication**
   Misunderstandings can trigger fights. If you think someone is ignoring you, you might respond with anger. But maybe they never saw your message or were busy. When communication is unclear, conflict can grow.
3. **Lack of Resources**
   People may fight over limited time, money, or space. If a coworker takes credit for your work to gain a promotion, you might feel resentful. That can spark anger between the two of you.
4. **Diverse Values**
   Conflicts often arise when people hold different beliefs. Perhaps you have strong opinions on parenting methods, while a friend has opposing views. If you both feel you must convince the other, conflict can brew.
5. **Unresolved Past Issues**
   Old hurts or grudges can show up in current conflicts. You might react with more anger than a situation deserves because it reminds you of past pain.

Recognizing these root causes can help you pick a plan to solve the conflict. If the problem is a resources issue, for instance, you can focus on finding a fair way to share or substitute. If it is a communication issue, you can use tools from the previous chapter to speak and listen more clearly.

---

## Conflict Resolution Styles

Not everyone solves problems in the same way. In general, there are five common styles people use in conflicts:

1. **Avoidance**: They run from the problem. They might pretend it does not exist or wait for it to go away on its own.
2. **Accommodation**: They give in to keep the peace. They might agree with whatever the other side wants, even if they feel upset inside.
3. **Competition**: They see the conflict as a contest to win, even if it hurts the other person.
4. **Compromise**: They meet in the middle. Both sides give up something to reach a solution.
5. **Collaboration**: They work together to find a win-win outcome that satisfies everyone as much as possible.

Each style can be useful in certain situations. Avoidance might be fine for very small problems that truly do not matter. Accommodation might be kind in an emergency to calm things down. However, if you always avoid or accommodate, you might end up with built-up resentment. Competition can be helpful if you must stand up for a clear boundary, but it can harm relationships if used too often.

Most of the time, compromise or collaboration help preserve relationships and manage anger. They require open communication, respect, and a willingness to see things from the other side's point of view. Let us look at some methods for making these approaches work in practice.

---

## Step 1: Calm Down Before You Start

When you try to solve a conflict in the middle of a heated moment, anger can cloud your judgment. You might say things you regret later or ignore what the other person says. If possible, take a quick break to calm yourself before trying to resolve the conflict. This could mean:

- Stepping outside for fresh air
- Doing a brief deep breathing exercise
- Counting to ten or twenty in your head
- Using a calm, simple phrase to ground yourself (like "I can handle this.")

Once you feel your body relax, you can come back to the discussion with a clearer mind. This lowers the chance of yelling or name-calling. If the other person is also angry, suggest they take a moment to cool down too. Just be sure to set a time to return to the conversation, so they do not feel you are avoiding the issue.

---

## Step 2: Define the Problem

If you jump straight to solutions without defining the problem, you risk solving the wrong issue. Conflicts can have many parts. Take a moment to figure out what is really happening. For example, imagine you and your spouse argue a lot about cooking dinner. On the surface, it might look like the fight is about food. But if you ask each other questions, you might learn that the deeper problem is feeling unappreciated. One person might say, "I cook every night and you never notice my effort."

By pinpointing that the main issue is recognition, you can address that more effectively. You might decide to thank each other for your contributions, or take turns cooking, or plan a special meal once a week. If you just argue about the dinner menu without talking about feeling unappreciated, you might not fix the root cause.

---

## Step 3: Listen to Each Other's Perspectives

This is where active listening from Chapter 7 comes into play. Give each side a chance to speak without interruption. Encourage them to share how they see the problem and why it matters to them. Then restate their points to ensure you understand. For instance:

- You: "So, you feel like you are the one doing most of the housework, and you are overwhelmed because you never get a break?"
- Other Person: "Yes, that is right. And I feel frustrated when I come home and see dishes piled up after I have already cleaned the kitchen."

By showing that you hear them, you can reduce some of their anger. They might also be more willing to listen to your perspective afterward. If both sides feel heard, the conflict is already on better footing.

---

## Step 4: Brainstorm Possible Solutions

Once you have a clear grasp of the issue, list as many possible solutions as you can think of. Do not worry if some ideas seem odd at first. The goal is to open up options. For example:

- Split chores by day (one person does Monday, Wednesday, Friday; the other does Tuesday, Thursday, Saturday).
- Assign each person a specific task all the time (one does cooking, the other cleans).
- Order takeout a couple of nights a week if it fits the budget.
- Ask other family members or roommates to help with certain tasks.
- Use a chore calendar or app to keep track of responsibilities.

Allow the other side to suggest ideas, too. Try not to shoot down any idea right away. Write everything down. Later, you can look at the list and see which ideas might be realistic.

---

## Step 5: Evaluate the Options and Choose

Now it is time to pick a solution or combine several ideas into one plan. Discuss each option's pros and cons. Ask questions like:

- Does this meet the main need each person mentioned?
- Is it fair for both sides?
- Do we have the resources (time, money, skills) to make this solution work?

- Will this plan cause new problems?

Sometimes, you will find a single option that both sides like. Other times, you might blend two or more ideas. If you cannot fully agree, you might aim for a compromise: each side gives up part of what they want but gains something else. Let us say you want more time to yourself, and the other person wants more help with tasks. A compromise might be that you spend 30 minutes each day helping, but in return, you get Saturday morning for personal activities.

---

## Step 6: Plan the Next Steps

Just picking a solution is not enough. You need to decide how you will carry it out. Be as clear as possible:

- Who will do what?
- When will each step happen?
- Do you need to schedule follow-up talks to see how it is going?

For instance, if you decide to split chores by day, you might note on a calendar whose turn it is. You could plan a short check-in every Sunday night to see if the plan is working. By breaking the solution into clear tasks, you avoid confusion that can lead to new conflicts. Each person knows exactly what is expected and when.

---

## Step 7: Follow Up and Adjust

Many solutions need fine-tuning. After trying your plan for a week or two, talk again to see what is working and what is not. You might find the plan is perfect as is. Or you might discover small issues that need fixing. For example, if you agreed to share cooking duties but realized one person gets home later, you might shift dinner prep to the other person on weekdays and switch on weekends.

It is normal for conflicts to need ongoing attention, especially if they are about daily tasks, time management, or shared resources. Checking in periodically helps catch frustrations early before they explode into full anger again.

## Handling Strong Emotions

Even with a good conflict-resolution plan, anger can still show up. Here are a few steps to handle strong emotions:

1. **Pause and Breathe**
   If you feel your anger rising, use a brief pause. Take deep breaths and remind yourself, "I am trying to solve this, not fight."
2. **Speak Up**
   If the other person says something that triggers you, calmly say, "That comment feels hurtful. Could you please clarify what you mean?" This invites them to explain instead of letting your anger escalate.
3. **Take Short Breaks**
   If the talk gets too heated, agree on a 10-minute break. Use that time to walk around, drink water, or do some breathing exercises. Then return when calmer.
4. **Stay Respectful**
   Even if you disagree, avoid calling each other names or insulting each other's character. Stick to describing behaviors, not attacking the person.

Keeping these practices in mind helps keep conflicts on track. You might still feel upset, but you can channel those feelings into finding solutions rather than hurling insults.

## When Conflicts Involve More Than Two People

Sometimes, conflicts involve an entire group—like a work team or several family members. In those cases, you can adapt the steps above:

- **Choose a Facilitator**: If possible, pick someone neutral to guide the discussion and keep order.
- **Set Ground Rules**: Everyone might agree on rules like no interrupting, no name-calling, and a time limit for each speaker.
- **Let Each Person Speak**: Give each person a turn to explain their concerns without being cut off.

- **Group Brainstorming**: Encourage all members to suggest solutions. Write them on a whiteboard or paper.
- **Vote or Reach a Group Agreement**: Decide which solution the majority can support. If there is strong opposition, see if you can modify the plan to address it.

Group conflicts can be tricky because there are more opinions and emotions involved. However, the same idea applies: calm the situation, define the problem, hear all sides, brainstorm, pick a plan, and follow up.

---

## Dealing with Ongoing Disagreements

Some conflicts do not end with one conversation. You might be dealing with a person who repeats the same behavior over and over. Or you might have big value-based disagreements that do not have an easy fix. Here are some tips:

- **Set Boundaries**: If the conflict involves hurtful actions, such as yelling or disrespect, you can say, "I will not engage if you use that tone. I am willing to talk when we can both stay respectful."
- **Seek Mediation**: A trained mediator can help people who clash repeatedly. They are skilled at guiding tough conversations and helping each side see the other's perspective.
- **Decide How Much to Engage**: In some cases, you may choose to reduce contact if the conflict partner is not willing to change. This might be a last resort if the situation seriously harms your well-being.
- **Accept Partial Solutions**: Sometimes you will not see eye to eye on everything. If you can find small points of agreement that ease the anger, that may be enough to live with relative peace.

It can be frustrating to deal with ongoing disagreements, but these steps can keep anger from running the show. You can still protect your mental health and show respect, even if the other person is difficult.

---

## Recognizing When Issues Are Too Large

Some conflicts cannot be resolved with simple steps. This can happen if there is deep abuse, an unsafe environment, or a major mismatch in core values. In those extreme cases, your safety and well-being come first. No amount of calm conversation can fix a situation where one party is determined to harm the other or refuses to respect basic boundaries.

If you are in a harmful situation, seek help from professionals, community resources, or trusted friends. Conflict resolution methods are designed for disagreements in which both sides have some willingness to cooperate or at least respect each other's rights. They are not meant to fix serious abuse or threats of harm.

---

## Teaching Conflict Resolution to Children

If you have children, teaching them how to solve conflicts calmly can shape how they deal with anger as they grow. Here are some child-friendly methods:

- **Use Simple Words**: Say, "If you are upset, tell your sibling, 'I do not like that. Please stop.'"
- **Encourage Taking Turns**: If they fight over a toy, have a timer that gives each child a set amount of playtime with the toy before switching.
- **Coach Them Through Apologies**: Show them how to say "I am sorry for pushing you" and to say what they will do next time (like, "I will use my words instead of pushing").
- **Praise Team Efforts**: If they manage to solve a small argument on their own, give them a positive comment. For example, "I saw how you both worked out a plan to share the crayons. Great job talking it through."

Teaching children these skills early can reduce anger in your home. It also sets them up to handle bigger conflicts in school or later in life.

---

## Benefits of Conflict Resolution

When you approach conflicts with a plan:

- **Less Anger Build-Up**: You nip problems in the bud before they turn into full-blown rage.
- **More Trust in Relationships**: People around you learn that even when you disagree, you will listen and try to solve the issue fairly.
- **Stronger Communication Skills**: You practice expressing your needs clearly, which can help with all areas of life—work, friendships, family.
- **Greater Confidence**: Each time you successfully solve a conflict, you show yourself that you can handle tense situations without losing your cool.

Over time, these benefits can improve your overall mood and reduce stress. You no longer carry the weight of unresolved anger.

## Quick Conflict-Solving Checklists

Here are two short checklists you can keep in mind:

### Checklist 1: During a Conflict

1. Calm yourself.
2. Define the core issue.
3. Listen to the other side.
4. Brainstorm solutions together.
5. Pick and plan an option.
6. Stay respectful and focused.

### Checklist 2: After a Conflict

1. Review the outcome.
2. Check how well the plan is working.
3. Make changes if needed.
4. Look at your own actions—do you need to apologize or adjust your behavior?
5. Thank the other person if they worked with you kindly.
6. Note what you learned for next time.

Keeping these steps in mind can help you stay organized when a conflict pops up.

## Realistic Expectations

Conflict resolution does not guarantee that everyone ends up thrilled. It aims to find a workable solution that keeps relationships intact and anger at manageable levels. Sometimes, the best you can do is create a plan that is fair enough for everyone to live with, even if it is not perfect. Accepting this can lower frustration. It is fine if a solution is "good enough" rather than flawless.

## Moving Toward Better Outcomes

Conflicts do not have to tear you apart or leave you boiling with anger. By following clear steps—calming down, defining the issue, listening fully, brainstorming, and picking a plan—you can address problems in a structured way. This method respects both sides and encourages a more positive result.

As you practice these methods, you might see that conflicts become less scary. You might even feel a sense of relief when you can talk through disagreements without yelling or silent resentment. Each solved conflict can bring a sense of peace and mutual respect. And in the bigger picture, these skills can help you maintain healthier relationships and keep your own anger under better control.

Up next, we will explore how to handle stress and anger together. Stress and anger often feed each other, so learning to manage stress can reduce your risk of outbursts. By combining conflict-resolution skills with smart stress management, you can create a more stable and calm day-to-day life.

# Chapter 9: Handling Stress and Anger

Stress is a major factor behind anger. When you feel pulled in many directions, it is easier for your temper to flare. Even small problems can seem huge if your mind and body are already under tension. In this chapter, we will look at why stress makes anger worse, how to lower daily tension, and what to do when stress threatens to push you into an angry outburst. By understanding the link between stress and anger, you can lessen the load and keep yourself calmer in tough moments.

---

## Recognizing the Connection Between Stress and Anger

Stress arises when you have too many demands or when life events feel overwhelming. You might feel this way when work deadlines stack up, when a loved one is ill, or when you are juggling many tasks at once. During stressful periods, anger is more likely because your emotional reserves are drained. If you imagine that you have an internal "stress container," each stressful event adds to it. Eventually, even a minor annoyance can cause the container to overflow in anger.

- **Physical Symptoms**: Stress can cause headaches, stomach aches, muscle tension, and fatigue. These make you more vulnerable to lashing out when something irritates you.
- **Emotional Strain**: Long-term stress can lead to sadness, worry, or irritability. These feelings pile on top of each other, creating a fragile mood where anger can easily surface.
- **Sense of Pressure**: When you believe you have no time or energy left, the smallest extra request from a coworker or family member can feel unbearable, triggering frustration or rage.

By acknowledging that your anger levels may rise during stressful times, you can take steps to manage both stress and anger at the same time.

---

## Everyday Sources of Stress

Daily stress can come from many places:

1. **Work Pressures**: A demanding boss, tight deadlines, or heavy workloads can leave you tense and jumpy. You might feel angry if you think your efforts are not recognized or if colleagues are not pulling their weight.
2. **Financial Worries**: Concerns over bills, debt, or future savings can loom in your mind. You might feel anger toward yourself for not earning more or toward others you see as more fortunate.
3. **Family Tensions**: Arguments at home, caring for children or aging parents, or dealing with misunderstandings between relatives can all raise stress. You may find that you have little personal space, which can lead to anger.
4. **Social Commitments**: Too many invitations or obligations, even pleasant ones, can cause burnout. If you seldom have time to relax, you might lash out over silly matters.
5. **Health Challenges**: Chronic pain or illnesses can sap your energy. Even temporary health concerns can disrupt your usual routine. Feeling unwell can make it harder to keep your temper under control.

Seeing these common sources of stress can help you figure out where you need to make changes. You can also spot which areas are most likely to set off your anger, giving you clues about where to place your efforts.

---

## Signs That Stress Is Building Up

Stress tends to pile up over time. You may not notice it until you are on the edge of an angry eruption. Here are some clues that stress is rising:

- **Tiredness**: You feel drained no matter how much sleep you get. Waking up in the morning already exhausted might be a sign you are carrying too much stress.
- **Trouble Concentrating**: You cannot focus on tasks you used to handle easily. Your mind jumps from one worry to another.
- **Frequent Mood Swings**: You switch quickly from feeling fine to feeling upset or sad.

- **Little Joy in Activities**: Things you used to find fun or meaningful feel dull.
- **Physical Discomfort**: You have tight muscles, frequent headaches, back pain, or other physical aches without a clear medical cause.

If you notice these signals, it is wise to pause and see what might be causing your stress levels to climb. By acting early, you can keep anger from spiking later on.

---

## Healthy Ways to Lower Daily Stress

Lowering your stress does not mean removing every challenge in life. Instead, it involves finding methods to handle those challenges without feeling overwhelmed. Below are some suggestions:

1. **Plan and Prioritize**
   Make a short list each day of what must be done, what can wait, and what is optional. Tackle the most pressing tasks first so they do not hover over you all day. Letting go of lower-priority items can ease stress, which lowers your risk of anger later.
2. **Take Short Breaks**
   Even five minutes away from a task can help you calm down. Stand up, stretch your arms, get some fresh air, or sip water. These small pauses can prevent stress from building to a harmful level.
3. **Protect Your Sleep**
   Lack of rest makes stress worse and makes it harder to control your temper. Set a bedtime that allows for enough rest. Avoid screens right before bed. If worry keeps you awake, write down your concerns on paper and promise yourself you will revisit them in the morning.
4. **Stay Active if You Can**
   Physical activity can help release tension. A simple walk, a home exercise routine, or a gentle activity can ease stress hormones in your body. You do not have to do intense workouts if that does not suit you—any movement is helpful.
5. **Mindful Breathing**
   Try a simple breathing exercise when you feel tension rise. Inhale slowly,

pause for a moment, and exhale gently. Repeat a few times. This can reset your body's stress response, reducing the chance of an angry burst.
6. **Talk It Out**
Sometimes sharing your stress with a trusted friend, a counselor, or a family member can bring relief. Speaking your worries can help you see solutions or gain support. If you keep your troubles silent, they often grow in your head, feeding stress.

These steps may appear small, but they can bring significant relief if done regularly. Lower overall stress means less chance of anger controlling your behavior.

---

## Setting Boundaries to Prevent Overload

One cause of stress is taking on too many responsibilities. It may be hard for women to say "no" when asked for help. You might feel guilty or fear letting someone down. However, always saying "yes" can stretch you too thin, leading to chronic stress and anger outbursts. Setting boundaries is an act of respect for yourself and for others. Consider these tips:

1. **Determine What You Can Handle**
Look at your current tasks—home chores, work, child care, community obligations—and see if you can truly manage them. If not, you need to lighten the load.
2. **Practice Saying "No" Politely**
You do not have to justify yourself in detail. A simple, "I'm sorry, but I can't take this on right now," is enough. If you want, you can offer an alternative, like, "I can help next month, but not this week."
3. **Delegate or Ask for Help**
If you cannot remove a task, see if you can share it. Ask a friend to babysit for an afternoon, or ask your partner to handle some errands. Delegation does not mean you are lazy; it means you recognize you have limits.
4. **Set Time Limits**
If someone keeps calling you to chat for hours, it might eat into the time you need for other tasks. Let them know, "I have about ten minutes to talk now, then I have to do something else." This prevents your schedule from being hijacked.

By setting these kinds of boundaries, you guard your energy and reduce stress, which can keep anger from boiling over later. You might feel awkward at first, but with practice, you can learn to say "no" when you must.

---

## Handling Stressful Moments on the Spot

Even with a good routine, stress can appear suddenly—a traffic jam, a rude comment, or a last-minute work request. Knowing how to handle it in the moment can stop anger from erupting. Here are some quick tactics:

1. **Ground Yourself**
   Pay attention to your senses. Notice three things you can see, two things you can hear, and one thing you can feel. This pulls your mind away from stressful thoughts and into the present moment.
2. **Use Quick Calming Words**
   Silently repeat a short phrase, such as "I can handle this," or "Stay calm," a few times. This mental pattern can keep your thoughts from spiraling.
3. **Pause Before Responding**
   If someone says something upsetting, take a breath before reacting. Count to three in your mind. This brief pause can keep anger from taking over.
4. **Accept What You Cannot Control**
   If you are stuck in a traffic jam, your anger will not make the cars move faster. In that case, it might help to switch to music you like or a calming audio program. By focusing on what you can control—your internal state—you might reduce stress about the things you cannot change.

Applying these quick tools during stressful moments can be the difference between a manageable annoyance and a full-on angry meltdown.

---

## The Role of Mindset in Stress and Anger

How you think about stress can shape how strongly it affects you. Certain thinking habits fuel stress, which then leads to anger. Examples include:

- **Catastrophic Thinking**: Believing that one setback means everything will fall apart.
- **Perfectionism**: Demanding that you handle every detail flawlessly, leaving no room for mistakes or rest.
- **Negative Filtering**: Focusing only on the bad parts of your day while ignoring any good parts.

Changing these patterns can lower your stress. Instead of telling yourself, "This is a disaster; I'll never fix it," you could try, "This is tough, but I can find a way through." Instead of believing "I must be perfect at all times," say, "I'll do my best and learn from mistakes." Shifting your mindset does not mean ignoring real problems, but it does mean easing unneeded pressure.

---

## Stress-Reduction Methods Outside the Home

Sometimes the place that causes the most stress is not your home but somewhere else—like your workplace or school. You can still try certain methods to stay calm:

1. **Use Break Spaces**
   If your workplace has a lounge or quiet corner, spend a few minutes there to decompress. Even a quick break can reset your stress levels.
2. **Stay Organized**
   Keep your workspace tidy if possible. A cluttered desk or confusing schedule can add to stress. If you can create a simple system—like labeled folders, a clear to-do list—you lower mental chaos.
3. **Communicate Needs**
   If your boss or coworkers are piling tasks on you, politely let them know when you are at capacity. If you cannot meet a deadline without sacrificing all your personal time, say so. This helps manage expectations.
4. **Take Walks**
   If you can, walk for a few minutes around your building or down the street. This quick movement can calm your mind. You can also do small stretches right at your desk if walking is not an option.
5. **Avoid Toxic Talk**
   Office gossip or harsh criticism can raise stress. You do not have to join

every discussion. If the talk is negative, you can excuse yourself or change the subject.

Bringing your own stress-lowering habits into the workplace can help you keep your temper in check, even under pressure.

---

## Stress and Physical Health

When stress builds up, it affects your body. Over time, chronic stress can:

- Weaken your immune system
- Raise your blood pressure
- Contribute to trouble sleeping
- Worsen aches or pains
- Impact your appetite and digestion

All of these issues can make you more prone to anger outbursts. For instance, if you have not slept well for days, you will probably have less patience. If you are often ill or in pain, that discomfort can make small problems feel bigger. Taking care of your health—through a balanced diet, regular rest, moderate exercise if possible, and check-ups—gives your mind a better chance to remain calm.

---

## Emotional Release for Stress Relief

Stress and anger can build when you do not let out strong emotions safely. If you are in a stressful time, you might try some form of emotional release:

1. **Cry in Private**
   A good cry can be a release if you have been holding back sadness. It may not fix the stressful situation, but it can ease internal tension.
2. **Laugh it Off**
   Sometimes, finding something humorous—a funny video, a comic strip, or a silly story—can help your body release stress through laughter.
3. **Write Freely**
   Fill a page with all your worries and fears. You do not have to keep it. Tear

it up or delete it afterward if you like. The act of writing can lower the pressure in your mind.
4. **Safe Anger Outlets**
As discussed in a previous chapter, activities like punching a pillow, going for a run, or shouting where nobody else is disturbed can help discharge pent-up anger from stress.

These short-term releases can help you feel lighter, though you should also look for ways to solve ongoing stress sources if possible.

---

## Accepting What You Cannot Fix Immediately

Life events such as losing a job, dealing with serious health problems, or facing relationship breakups can bring massive stress that cannot be solved right away. In these cases, you may feel stuck, leading to anger at yourself, others, or the situation. While you cannot snap your fingers and fix everything, you can:

- **Focus on What Is Still in Your Control**
  You might not fix the big problem overnight, but you can handle small steps—updating your resume, scheduling a doctor's visit, or seeking legal help if needed.
- **Lean on Support**
  Friends, family, community groups, or counselors can offer both emotional and practical help. It is not weak to ask for assistance.
- **Practice Self-Compassion**
  Treat yourself with kindness. Avoid harsh self-criticism like "I should be stronger." Remind yourself you are doing your best under tough circumstances.
- **Give Yourself Breaks**
  Even during major stress, allow moments of peace—listening to soothing music, strolling outside, or enjoying a calming hobby if you can.

Accepting what you cannot fix instantly does not mean giving up. It means recognizing that some solutions take time. While you work through that period, treating yourself gently can keep your stress from turning into constant anger.

---

## Stress Management for Busy Schedules

Many women say they do not have the time to calm down. Between work, family, and daily chores, they feel there is no space for self-care. Yet even a few minutes a day can make a difference. Consider these ideas:

1. **Morning Minute**
   Before diving into your tasks, spend one minute sitting quietly. Breathe slowly and set a small intention, like "I will be gentle with myself today."
2. **Break Alarms**
   If possible, set an alarm on your phone to remind you to take a short pause every two hours. Stretch your arms, roll your shoulders, and breathe. This keeps stress from piling up.
3. **Stacking Habits**
   Combine a calming habit with a daily routine. For example, while waiting for your coffee, do a 30-second breathing practice. Or while brushing your teeth, think of one thing you feel thankful for.
4. **Mini-Relaxation Before Bed**
   Spend two minutes doing a simple body scan. Start from your toes and move upward, telling each body part to relax. This helps you wind down and can lead to better sleep.

Even if these actions seem small, they create a buffer that can stop stress from taking over your day.

---

## Recognizing Stress in Others

If you see a friend or family member getting angry often, they might also be under stress. You can encourage them to try some of the ideas listed here. However, remember you cannot force anyone to change their habits. You can offer understanding and empathy, which sometimes helps them feel less alone. If their stress leads to anger directed at you in hurtful ways, you may need to set boundaries or seek support to protect your own well-being.

---

## Warning Signs of Burnout

Burnout is a state of chronic stress that leaves you feeling drained and unable to cope. Signs of burnout include:

- **Feeling Detached**: You might stop caring about work, family, or tasks that once mattered.
- **Constant Tiredness**: No matter how much rest you get, you are still wiped out.
- **Lowered Performance**: You have trouble keeping up with your usual tasks, missing deadlines or making errors.
- **Frequent Illness**: You get colds, headaches, or other minor illnesses more often.
- **Anger More Often**: You lash out at small things because you have no emotional fuel left.

If you sense burnout, consider speaking with a mental health professional or making a significant change in your routine if possible. Burnout can cause long-term harm if not addressed, and it can lead to constant anger that damages relationships.

---

## Putting It All Together

Stress does not have to control you. While you cannot remove every stressful thing in your life, you can make choices that lighten the burden:

- **Identify daily sources of stress**
- **Set boundaries to protect your time and energy**
- **Use brief methods (like breathing exercises) to release tension**
- **Work on changing unhelpful thought patterns**
- **Seek help if you feel overloaded or close to burnout**

By handling stress in a healthier way, you lower the chance of angry explosions that hurt you or the people around you. Anger often feeds on stress, so minimizing stress can cool that anger before it gets hot. In the next chapter, we will look at how to handle anger when juggling many tasks and roles in life. Balancing responsibilities can be a prime source of stress, but there are ways to manage those demands without letting frustration take over.

# Chapter 10: Managing Responsibilities and Anger

Many women face multiple roles and tasks each day. You might be a parent, a worker, a partner, a caregiver to older relatives, or a volunteer in your community. Often, these responsibilities compete for your time and energy. When you feel pulled in every direction, anger can flare up. You might snap at family members, resent your coworkers, or feel annoyed at friends who ask for your help. In this chapter, we will explore how to handle the sense of overload that comes with having many responsibilities, and how to keep that overload from turning into anger.

---

## The Pressure of Multiple Roles

Life can feel like a juggling act. Here are common responsibilities that many women take on:

1. **Work or Career**: You may spend eight or more hours at a job, dealing with deadlines, coworkers, and bosses.
2. **Home and Family**: Cooking, cleaning, grocery shopping, helping children with homework, caring for pets, and more can fill the rest of your day.
3. **Personal Care**: Health check-ups, exercise, and finding moments for your own well-being are also important (though these often get overlooked).
4. **Social Connections**: Friends and community events can be a source of joy but also a demand on your limited time.
5. **Extended Family Duties**: Many women step in to help older relatives or relatives who are ill, adding another layer of responsibility.

When these tasks pile up, you may feel you have no time to breathe. This high level of stress can make you less patient. The result is often anger—at others for needing so much, or at yourself for not being able to handle it all perfectly.

---

## Recognizing Signs of Overload

Before anger takes over, watch for clues that your responsibilities are too heavy:

- **Constant Racing Thoughts**: Your mind jumps from one to-do item to another, never settling.
- **Feelings of Resentment**: You catch yourself thinking, "Why do I have to do everything around here?" or "No one understands how hard I work."
- **Frequent Mistakes or Forgetfulness**: You forget appointments or small tasks because you have too much on your plate.
- **Lack of Enjoyment**: Even if you once loved cooking or playing with your kids, you now feel burdened or annoyed by these activities.
- **Physical Tension**: Tight shoulders, a stiff neck, or a clenched jaw that does not go away.

These signs suggest you may be stretching yourself too thin, making anger an ever-present risk.

---

## Learning to Say "No" to Extra Tasks

One major reason women feel overloaded is that they rarely turn down requests for help. While helping others can be kind, taking on too much can backfire. You end up exhausted and resentful. Here is how to practice saying "no" in a reasonable way:

1. **Pause Before You Agree**
   If someone asks you to help, avoid answering right away if you are not sure. Say, "Let me think about it and get back to you," or "I need to check my schedule." This stops you from saying "yes" out of habit.
2. **Evaluate the Request**
   Ask yourself: Do I truly have the time and energy to do this well? Will this conflict with other important tasks or my self-care? If it does, it might be better to politely decline.
3. **Give a Clear but Kind Response**
   You can say, "I'm sorry, but I'm at my limit and can't help this time," or "I wish I could help, but I'm not free right now." If you want, you can offer a smaller form of help, like a quick piece of advice rather than fully taking on their request.
4. **Stand Firm**
   Some people might push for a "yes." Repeating your refusal is sometimes necessary. "I really can't take this on, I'm sorry." You do not have to explain yourself in detail.

These steps can prevent new responsibilities from piling on and fueling your anger later. Remember: refusing a request does not mean you are selfish. It means you respect your limits so you can be at your best for the tasks you have already chosen.

---

## Delegating or Sharing Tasks

If your tasks are already too numerous, consider how to share the load:

1. **At Home**
   If you live with others, discuss which chores or errands they can take on. Even children can help with age-appropriate jobs like folding laundry or tidying their rooms. A partner can shop for groceries or cook certain meals if they have the time.
2. **At Work**
   If you are a team leader, see if tasks can be assigned to others. If you are not in charge, you can still speak to your manager about your current workload. Sometimes, coworkers can split responsibilities if asked.
3. **With Friends**
   If you have close friends you trust, you can trade tasks, like babysitting each other's children, sharing rides, or cooking meals for each other on busy nights.
4. **Paid Services**
   If you can afford it, you might hire help, such as a cleaning person who comes once a month or a part-time nanny. Even a small amount of hired help can free up your time and lower stress.

By letting others pitch in, you can ease your anger risk. The goal is not to "dump" your duties but to find a fair distribution among the people in your life or to use services within your means.

---

## Organizing Your Tasks

Poor organization can make responsibilities seem more massive than they are. By structuring your to-do list, you can feel more in control and less prone to anger:

1. **Make a Master List**
   Write down every task you need or want to do. This can clear your head. Then categorize tasks by importance or by the day they must be done.
2. **Use a Calendar**
   Put deadlines, appointments, and reminders on a calendar. Whether it is a paper planner or a digital app, seeing tasks laid out by day or week can keep you from feeling overwhelmed.
3. **Break Down Big Tasks**
   If you have a big project, split it into smaller steps. Complete one step at a time. This prevents the feeling that you have an endless mountain to climb.
4. **Schedule Rest and Fun**
   If you do not set aside time for yourself, those moments never happen. Mark blocks of downtime in your planner, even if they are brief. Treat them like real appointments that you do not want to cancel.
5. **Review and Adjust**
   Each week, look back at what worked and what did not. If your schedule is still too full, decide what to remove or postpone.

Good organization helps you see which tasks are truly urgent and which can wait. This method also reduces the frantic feeling that triggers anger when you are trying to do everything at once.

---

## Setting Realistic Expectations

Sometimes anger comes from expecting yourself to handle tasks at an impossible level. For example, you might insist on cooking a three-course meal each night or keeping your home spotless. Meanwhile, you hold down a full-time job and care for children. Such high expectations can set you up for frustration. Instead:

- **Ask, "Is this standard necessary?"** Maybe quick meals with simple ingredients are fine on busy nights. A clean-enough living space might be better than a perfectly neat one if it helps you stay calm.
- **Forgive Yourself for Imperfections**: Mistakes happen. Dinners get burnt. You might forget a detail on a school form. Instead of punishing yourself, see this as part of normal life.

- **Use Time-Saving Options**: Frozen vegetables, meal kits, or a weekly meal plan can save hours. Buying store-bought cookies for a bake sale might free you up to rest. Let go of the idea that everything must be homemade from scratch.
- **Learn to Do Less, Better**: Focus on a few tasks that matter most and do them well. For the rest, aim for "good enough."

By lowering unrealistic demands on yourself, you cut down on stress and the anger that follows.

## Handling Guilt About Responsibilities

Women often experience guilt if they cannot meet all expectations—both their own and those of society, family, or employers. This guilt can turn into anger when you feel stuck doing more than you can manage. Some ways to handle guilt:

1. **Identify the Source**
   Are you feeling guilty because you grew up believing a "good mother" or "good daughter" does certain things? Ask if these beliefs are flexible. Times change, family roles change, and you might be allowed to share tasks or do them differently.
2. **Talk Back to Guilt**
   When you hear that guilty voice in your head, respond gently. For example, "I may not be able to take my child to every single after-school activity, but I do spend quality time with them at home." This balanced view can reduce guilt.
3. **Seek Support**
   Share your feelings with a friend or counselor. Hearing that others also face these struggles might ease your sense of shame. They may offer ideas to handle things more smoothly.

Guilt can sap your energy, leaving you on edge. By challenging guilty thoughts, you regain emotional balance and protect yourself from angry outbursts.

## Balancing Work and Home

Combining a job with family life is a common source of anger and stress. You might feel torn between professional demands and personal duties. Here are some ways to lessen that tension:

1. **Set Clear Work-Home Boundaries**
   If possible, do not bring work tasks or emails into your family time. If you work from home, designate a specific spot or certain hours for work. This helps you be present at home and reduces distractions that cause stress.
2. **Plan Routines**
   Establish a predictable morning and evening routine. If you know exactly how much time you need to prepare for work, cook, help with homework, and relax, you are less likely to feel rushed and angry.
3. **Communicate with Your Boss**
   If your job is flexible, let your boss know you may need to leave early for a child's event or handle a family matter. Plan how you will make up that time. Honest communication can prevent last-minute crises.
4. **Avoid Perfection at Work**
   You can still do a good job without staying extra hours every day or taking on tasks beyond your role. If you are near burnout, speak up. Pushing yourself too hard at work may lead to anger that spills over into your home life.
5. **Team Up with Your Family**
   Let your partner and kids know your work challenges. This can help them understand why you might need quiet time or why you might not always be available right away. They can support you, and you can do the same for them.

Balancing work and home is not always easy, but small adjustments can go a long way toward preventing anger explosions.

---

## Avoiding Comparisons

Comparing yourself to others can fuel anger and frustration. You might see a neighbor or coworker who seems to "have it all together" and wonder why you struggle. But keep in mind:

- People often hide their own struggles. Social media or casual conversations may not reveal the stress they deal with behind the scenes.
- Your life situation and strengths are unique to you. What works for another person might not fit your circumstances.
- Comparison can lead to envy or shame, which can turn into anger toward yourself or others.

Instead, focus on your own progress. If you are meeting your responsibilities in a way that suits you and the people who rely on you, that is what matters.

---

## Reclaiming Personal Time

When you have many responsibilities, personal time is often the first thing to go. Yet skipping personal time can build anger, as you feel your own needs are ignored. Try to carve out moments just for yourself:

1. **Schedule It**
   Treat personal time as an appointment. Whether it is 15 minutes in the morning or a half-hour before bed, mark it down so you do not forget.
2. **Choose an Activity That Soothes You**
   This could be reading, listening to music, doing a puzzle, or a hobby that you enjoy. You do not need a long stretch of time to gain benefits—consistency is key.
3. **Ask for Support**
   Tell family members that this time is important for you. Ask them not to disturb you unless there is an emergency. With children, set them up with an activity they can do on their own safely, or swap babysitting duties with a friend.
4. **Unplug from Devices**
   Electronic devices can flood you with demands, from work emails to social media updates. Try to turn them off or silence them during your personal time.

Taking even a small window for yourself can recharge you, helping you stay patient with the many tasks you face.

---

## Dealing with Unexpected Problems

Even with careful planning, unexpected events can pop up—an appliance breaks, a child falls ill, or a work project hits a snag. These can topple your balanced schedule. To handle these moments:

- **Reorder Tasks**
  Decide which tasks must still happen today, and which can wait. It might mean postponing a less urgent chore to handle the new emergency.
- **Ask for Backup**
  If your child is sick, see if a friend or relative can pick up groceries for you. If a project is stuck at work, talk with your team right away.
- **Stay Flexible in Your Mindset**
  Remind yourself that life can be unpredictable. The more you can adapt your schedule, the less stress and anger you will feel.
- **Use Quick Stress Tools**
  In the chaos of a sudden problem, pause to do deep breathing or a grounding exercise. This keeps anger from spiraling out of control.

These steps can keep an unexpected crisis from pushing you past your limit into anger overload.

---

## Communicating Your Limits

Family members, coworkers, and friends cannot read your mind. If you never tell them you are overloaded, they might keep expecting you to handle things. Be open about your limits:

1. **State the Facts**
   "I have three projects due this week, and I'm already working late hours."
2. **Share Feelings Briefly**
   "I feel overwhelmed because I have no downtime."
3. **Offer a Suggestion**
   "Could we shift the deadline on one project or get more help on it? Otherwise, I won't finish on time."

This direct approach is more effective than silently stewing in anger, hoping others will notice your distress. By speaking up, you give them a chance to help or find solutions.

## Acknowledging Your Progress

When you do manage your responsibilities without letting anger get the best of you, note that progress. Many women overlook their successes because they focus on what still needs to be done. Try to pause once in a while to say, "I handled a busy day, fed the kids, and met my work deadline. I'm doing all right." This small acknowledgment can boost your mood and reduce the pressure that feeds anger.

---

## Handling Anger When You Feel Unappreciated

Sometimes, you might do a large share of tasks, yet feel no one sees your efforts. This lack of appreciation can lead to resentment:

- **Communicate the Feeling**
  Tell your family or colleagues, "I'd like my work to be noticed. It motivates me when my efforts are recognized."
- **Reward Yourself**
  If others do not give thanks, you can still decide to do something nice for yourself when you complete a tough task—like reading a favorite book for 20 minutes, or preparing a snack you enjoy.
- **Spread Out the Responsibilities**
  Sometimes, consistent help from others leads them to realize how much you do. If you stop taking on extra tasks, they might see the gap and appreciate the work that was once done quietly.
- **Consider an Honest Talk**
  If the lack of appreciation feels deep, have a calm conversation about it. Explain how it affects your mood and your willingness to keep pushing yourself.

Feeling valued can reduce anger. Sometimes, all it takes is open communication or a reminder that you deserve kindness as well.

---

## Knowing When to Seek Professional Help

If you have adjusted your schedule, set boundaries, and tried to manage your tasks, but your anger remains high, it may be time to get outside help. Signs you might need professional support include:

- Anger outbursts happen daily or almost daily.
- You feel anxious or depressed in addition to feeling overwhelmed by tasks.
- You find yourself withdrawing from family and friends because you do not have the energy to talk.
- You have physical symptoms, such as ongoing insomnia, chronic headaches, or stomach trouble that do not improve.

A counselor or therapist can help you identify deeper patterns behind your anger. They can also help you refine your strategies for balancing responsibilities. If your workplace or family environment is especially demanding or tense, you might also explore coaching or mediation to create a healthier setup.

---

## Moving Forward with Balance

Managing many responsibilities is challenging, but it does not have to lead to constant anger. By setting clearer limits, organizing tasks, sharing duties, and allowing time for yourself, you can keep your emotional balance. Look for ways to simplify your load, and do not hesitate to speak up when you need help.

When you stop trying to do everything perfectly or alone, you reduce stress. This lowers the chance of snapping at loved ones or feeling trapped in your obligations. In the upcoming chapters, you will discover more tools to handle guilt, shame, and other feelings that can tie into anger. You will also find guidance on building self-worth and staying calm in the workplace. With each step, you can protect your peace of mind while still meeting life's many demands in a way that respects both your needs and those of others.

# Chapter 11: Moving Past Guilt and Shame

Guilt and shame often go hand in hand with anger. You might blame yourself for feeling angry, or you might look back on an angry outburst and wonder why you "could not keep it together." These feelings can weigh you down. They can also keep you stuck in a cycle: you get angry, then you feel guilty or ashamed about it, and then those feelings make you more tense or upset. In this chapter, we will talk about the difference between guilt and shame, why they appear with anger, and how to move beyond them so you can live with more peace and self-acceptance.

---

## Understanding Guilt vs. Shame

Guilt and shame are sometimes mentioned as if they mean the same thing, but they have important differences:

1. **Guilt**
   Guilt is the feeling that you did something wrong. When you feel guilty, you may think, "I made a mistake." Guilt can be helpful if it pushes you to make amends or change your behavior. For instance, if you shouted at a friend, guilt might lead you to apologize. However, guilt becomes unhealthy if it goes on and on without a path to fix the situation.
2. **Shame**
   Shame is deeper. It is the feeling that there is something wrong with who you are, rather than just something wrong with what you did. When you feel shame, you might think, "I am a bad person." Shame can be very heavy and make you want to hide or stay silent. It can also stop you from trying to improve things, because you believe you are beyond help.

When it comes to anger, some women feel guilty for shouting or acting in ways that might have harmed a relationship. Others feel shame, believing that being angry makes them flawed at a core level. Recognizing which feeling you have can be a first step to dealing with it in a healthier way.

---

## Why Guilt and Shame Follow Anger

Anger is often seen as a "bad" emotion, especially for women. There can be social or family rules that say you should stay calm and pleasant, never revealing an angry side. Because of this, showing anger might feel like a failure to be "good." You might sense judgment from the people around you, or you might sense an internal voice saying, "I should not act this way." Over time, this can create guilt (feeling regret for what happened) or shame (feeling that you are unworthy or damaged).

Also, anger can lead to behaviors that you regret later. You might slam a door or say something cruel in the heat of the moment. Once you cool down, you realize your words or actions hurt someone. This realization can trigger guilt or shame. If you do not know how to make things right or forgive yourself, those feelings can grow.

---

## The Harmful Cycle of Guilt, Shame, and Anger

When guilt or shame builds up, it can actually feed more anger. Picture this scenario: you yell at your child. Later, you feel guilty for losing your temper. But you do not talk about it or try to fix it, because you feel too ashamed. That guilt sits inside you, making you tense. The next time your child does something small that annoys you, you might blow up again because you are already on edge. Then the guilt repeats. This cycle can be tough to break.

Shame can also make you hide from people or avoid seeking help. If you think, "I must be a terrible person to feel this much anger," you might think no one can understand or support you. That sense of isolation can make anger more intense. You might feel lonely, and that loneliness can turn into more frustration or resentment.

---

## Learning to See Guilt as a Signal

Even though guilt can feel bad, it has a purpose: it tells you that your actions might not match your values. For example, if your value is to treat loved ones with kindness, yelling at them goes against that value. Guilt then pops up as an alert. Rather than seeing it as a punishment, you can learn to see guilt as a useful sign:

1. **Notice the Guilt**
   When you sense guilt, pause. Ask yourself, "Why am I feeling guilty?" Maybe you realize it is because you snapped at a friend or you made a harsh remark to a coworker.
2. **Check Your Values**
   Think about the behavior that caused your guilt. Which of your personal values was it going against? Maybe it was respect, honesty, or patience.
3. **Plan a Repair**
   Guilt is often an urge to fix the damage. This could mean apologizing, explaining your stress, or taking steps so it does not happen again. If you lost your temper, you might speak to the person calmly later and say, "I was upset, but I should not have shouted."
4. **Let Guilt Go**
   Once you have done what you can to make it right, learn to release the guilt. Holding onto it does not do anyone good.

By handling guilt as an action step instead of a weight that drags you down, you can break part of the cycle that leads to repeated anger outbursts.

---

## Challenging Shame Through Self-Compassion

Shame is more damaging than guilt because it touches your sense of worth as a person. Moving past shame often involves building compassion for yourself. If you have trouble showing kindness to yourself, picture how you would treat a dear friend going through the same struggle. You would not call them horrible or hopeless. You might offer a listening ear, remind them that everyone struggles sometimes, or help them see that mistakes do not define who they are.

Here are some ideas to tackle shame:

1. **Name the Feeling**
   When you feel that heavy sense of unworthiness, label it: "I am feeling shame right now." This can give you some mental distance.
2. **Ask What You Would Say to a Friend**
   Imagine a friend telling you they are ashamed of their anger. What would

you say to them? You might say, "We all get upset sometimes. It does not make you unlovable." Then apply those words to yourself.

3. **Recall Times You Did Good Things**
   Shame blinds you to your strengths. Try to remember moments when you acted with love, patience, or generosity. This can help balance the thoughts that you are "bad" because of an angry mistake.
4. **Seek Support**
   Talking to a counselor or joining a support group can help you see that your anger or mistakes do not define your entire being. Many women struggle with these same feelings, and hearing that you are not alone can lessen the force of shame.

Overcoming shame can take time, especially if you have carried it for years. But each small act of kindness toward yourself can loosen shame's grip on your heart.

---

## Releasing Guilt Through Apology and Action

Some women carry guilt about old episodes of anger. They might think about something they said long ago to a sibling or to a friend. If you still feel guilt for a past action, consider whether an apology or a gesture could bring closure. This does not mean you must contact someone who does not want to hear from you, but if it is possible to do so in a calm way, it might help both of you heal.

- **Make It Honest**: Say what you did, why you regret it, and how you plan to act differently in the future.
- **Do Not Demand Forgiveness**: The other person may still be hurt. They might need time. What matters is that you are owning your actions.
- **Back It Up with Change**: If you apologize but continue the same behavior, guilt will return. Aim for real changes in how you handle anger.

When you cannot apologize directly—maybe the person moved away or is no longer alive—you can find your own ritual of closure. This might involve writing a letter you do not send, talking to a counselor, or focusing on how you will treat others better in the present.

---

## Handling Self-Blame for Feeling Angry

Some women feel guilt or shame just for having anger at all, even if they never act on it. They might think a "good person" would never feel angry, so they label themselves as flawed. In reality, anger is a normal emotion. Telling yourself you are wrong to feel it can keep you locked in shame. Instead, accept that anger is part of being human. What you do with anger matters more than whether you feel it.

If you catch yourself thinking, "I should never feel angry," switch to, "Anger means something is bothering me. I can notice it and choose what to do next." This shift in viewpoint removes shame from the picture and turns anger into a signal that can guide you to address problems.

---

## Guilt, Shame, and Family Background

Sometimes, guilt and shame start in childhood. If you grew up in a home where adults scolded you for small mistakes or shamed you for expressing strong emotions, you might have learned to see yourself as "bad" whenever you felt angry. In other cases, you might have been punished severely if you showed any signs of anger. These early lessons can stick with you, even if you do not realize it.

It can help to think about where your guilt or shame started. Did someone in your life often say things like, "Only bad girls get angry" or "Stop crying, you have no right to be upset"? Did you see a family member who was always blaming themselves? By spotting these roots, you can remind yourself that you do not have to keep living by those old messages. You can choose new ways of thinking about anger and about your worth.

---

## Breaking the Silence

One big problem with guilt and shame is that they thrive in silence. When you feel ashamed, you may hide it, worried that people will think less of you. Yet talking about shame can loosen its hold. Even just telling a supportive friend, "I feel awful about how I behaved," can bring relief. They might say, "I have been there, too," which helps you realize you are not the only one who has made mistakes while angry.

If you do not have a friend you trust enough, a counselor or mental health professional can fill that role. They will not judge you for having anger or for regretting your actions. Their job is to help you see yourself in a kinder, more balanced way. The simple act of speaking guilt or shame aloud can start to release some of its power.

## Accepting Your Limits

Guilt often happens when you think you "should have done better" in a stressful moment. Shame can follow if you believe that "a better person would not have acted that way." But everyone has limits. We all reach points where our patience snaps or our ability to stay calm disappears, especially if we are under huge stress, lacking sleep, or feeling unwell.

Accepting your limits does not mean ignoring personal growth. Rather, it means recognizing that you are human. You can make mistakes and learn from them without labeling yourself as horrible. Acknowledging limits can also help you plan better. If you know you get irritable when you have not eaten, you can arrange quick meals or snacks to prevent that trigger. If you know large crowds stress you out, you can pace yourself at social events. By handling your limits, you reduce the times you act in anger and then feel guilty or ashamed afterward.

## Letting Go of Perfect Standards

Shame can also come from trying to be perfect. You might think you must be the perfect mother, partner, friend, or employee. When anger shows up, it feels like proof that you have failed in that perfect image. Letting go of perfect standards can help you see that anger does not make you a failure; it makes you human.

1. **Notice Unrealistic Beliefs**
   Do you believe a "good mother" never raises her voice? Do you believe a "strong worker" never asks for help? These beliefs can set you up for shame because they are not realistic.

2. **Allow for Bumps**
   Life is full of ups and downs. Sometimes you will handle anger well. Other times, you might slip. That is part of growth.
3. **Praise Small Progress**
   If you caught yourself and took a breath before yelling, that is progress from before. If you apologized sooner than usual, that is progress, too. These small steps can help you see that you are moving in a better direction instead of staying stuck.

By lowering the bar from "perfect" to "improving," you can prevent shame from taking over. You do not have to do everything right to be worthy.

---

## Forgiving Yourself

Self-forgiveness can feel awkward. Some people think that by forgiving themselves, they are letting themselves off the hook. But self-forgiveness is not about avoiding responsibility. It is about recognizing that you have made amends, learned from your mistakes, and deserve to move on. Holding onto guilt forever does not help anyone. In fact, it can cause more harm because you stay trapped in negative feelings.

Steps to self-forgiveness might include:

- **Admitting the Wrong**: Acknowledge to yourself what you did that caused guilt or shame.
- **Making It Right**: Apologize if you can. Repair any damage if possible.
- **Learning the Lesson**: What can you change so this does not keep happening? Maybe you use anger management techniques or talk to a therapist.
- **Releasing the Burden**: Remind yourself that you are not stuck in that past moment. You are allowed to move ahead with new knowledge.

Each time guilt or shame tries to creep back, tell yourself, "I have faced that event, made it right as best I can, and I am growing."

---

## Watching Out for Self-Punishment

Some women handle guilt and shame by punishing themselves in subtle ways. They might deprive themselves of rest or deny themselves simple pleasures because they feel they "do not deserve it." They might also stay in harmful relationships or refuse to seek better opportunities because they see themselves as unworthy. This self-punishment can keep shame alive.

If you notice self-punishing habits, try to replace them with self-care habits. For instance, if you catch yourself saying, "I should not go to lunch with friends because I acted badly last week," challenge that thought. Realize that everyone makes mistakes, and you have taken steps to fix yours. You can still enjoy time with friends. Over time, you break the pattern of punishing yourself for being human.

---

## Helpful Conversations About Guilt and Shame

Sometimes, openly talking about guilt and shame can help you and those close to you heal. If you often lose your temper with a family member, you could say:

- **"I feel bad about how I acted. I realize it hurt you."**
- **"I love you and want you to know my anger was about my stress, not about you personally."**
- **"I am working on handling my emotions better. If I slip up, please let me know gently."**

These statements show honesty, care, and a desire to grow. They also help the other person see that your anger is not a personal attack. Such talks can bring understanding that lowers shame for both sides.

---

## Moving Forward from Shame-Filled Identities

Some people carry a sense of shame for years, seeing themselves only as an "angry person." If that describes you, remember that anger is just one part of who you are. You might also be creative, caring, thoughtful, or funny. Shame narrows your view, but you can widen it again by noticing all parts of yourself:

- **List Your Positive Traits**: Write down qualities that you like about yourself, or things that friends have complimented you on. Keep this list where you can see it.
- **Set Kind Goals**: Decide on a small but kind act you can do each day, such as checking in with someone who seems lonely or doing a helpful task at home. Reminding yourself that you can do good things weakens the grip of shame.
- **Allow Compliments**: If someone praises you, try not to dismiss it. Accept the kind words and let them remind you that you are more than your flaws.

Over time, replacing a shame-based identity with a more balanced one can free you from the weight of believing you are "bad" just because you experience anger.

## Using Guilt and Shame as Growth Tools

You do not have to see guilt and shame as purely negative forces. When handled correctly, they can point you toward better choices:

- **Guilt** can show you where you need to fix a mistake or make amends. It can motivate you to learn better ways of reacting.
- **Shame** can be a sign that you need deeper healing or help. If you feel shame all the time, it might mean you carry past wounds that have not been addressed. Seeking therapy or a support group can open the door to true healing.

The key is to use these feelings for insight, not to remain stuck in them. Ask yourself, "What is this guilt or shame telling me? How can I respond in a way that helps me grow?"

## Step-by-Step Release

If you are tired of feeling guilt and shame after each angry moment, here is a simple outline to help you move forward:

1. **Identify**: Notice guilt or shame and name it.
2. **Reflect**: Ask what caused the feeling—did you act in a way that harmed someone, or are you just criticizing yourself unfairly?
3. **Act**: If you need to apologize, do so. If you need to change a routine or pattern, make a plan.
4. **Forgive**: Once you have done what you can, remind yourself that dwelling on guilt does not help. You have the right to grow past it.
5. **Support**: If shame feels overwhelming, reach out to a friend or professional.

Repeating this process whenever guilt or shame appears can weaken their hold. Over time, you learn to deal with these emotions without letting them define you.

## Looking Ahead

Moving past guilt and shame does not happen in a single day. It is more like learning a new way to see yourself—one that leaves space for mistakes, regrets, and also for healing and growth. Each time you handle a conflict in a calmer way, each time you offer a genuine apology and then let yourself move on, you make guilt and shame smaller in your life.

In the next chapter, we will talk about raising confidence and self-worth, which ties closely to letting go of guilt and shame. Feeling more confident can help you stand firm when anger arises. It can also give you courage to face difficult situations without labeling yourself as "bad." By learning to value yourself, you gain a defense against the heavy feelings that can swirl around anger.

Remember, guilt and shame do not have to be permanent shadows. They are feelings that can guide you toward better actions if you let them, but they are not meant to trap you. You can use them as signals, repair what you can, and move forward with respect for who you are, flaws included.

# Chapter 12: Raising Confidence and Self-Worth

Confidence and self-worth play a big role in how you handle anger. If you see yourself as unimportant or not capable, you might let small problems pile up until you explode. Or you might doubt your right to speak up when something bothers you, leading to buried anger that grows inside. Building confidence and self-worth helps you face problems sooner and express anger in healthier ways. It also makes it easier to hold onto a calm mind when others treat you poorly, because you know that you deserve respect. In this chapter, we will explore practical steps to grow a stronger sense of worth and self-belief.

---

## Why Confidence and Self-Worth Matter for Anger

When you do not believe in your own value, you might react in ways that fuel anger:

1. **Fear of Being Overlooked**
   If you think you are not good enough, you might assume others will ignore or dismiss you. This can make you extra sensitive to signs of disrespect, causing quick anger even if the person did not mean any harm.
2. **Difficulty Setting Boundaries**
   Without confidence, you may struggle to say "no" or speak up for your needs. Over time, this can lead to built-up resentment. You might blow up over something small because you have been holding your feelings in for so long.
3. **Taking Harsh Words to Heart**
   If someone criticizes or teases you, low self-worth can make those words feel like an attack on your entire identity. You might lash out, or you might turn the anger on yourself.
4. **Avoiding Responsibility**
   Sometimes low self-worth leads to avoiding mistakes at all costs. If you cannot accept that you can fail and still be okay, you might hide errors or blame others, which can create anger and conflict.

By boosting your sense of worth, you can address these problems more calmly. You will feel more comfortable standing up for yourself without yelling, and you will not crumble if someone points out an imperfection.

---

## Recognizing Low Self-Worth Patterns

You can spot signs of low self-worth in everyday thoughts or actions. For example:

- **Putting Yourself Down**: You might make jokes about how you are "useless" or "not smart enough," even if you do not fully believe it.
- **Brushing Off Compliments**: If someone praises you, you say, "It was nothing," or "Anybody could have done that," rather than accepting the compliment.
- **Comparing Yourself to Others**: You feel you do not measure up, thinking, "I am not as pretty, successful, or lovable as them."
- **Needing Constant Approval**: You wait for others to say you did well, or you worry about their opinion so much that it stops you from making decisions on your own.
- **Over-Apologizing**: You say "sorry" for things that are not your fault or beyond your control, as if you are always in the wrong.

Not everyone shows these signs the same way, but if you notice them often, it might be time to work on raising your confidence.

---

## Separating Your Actions from Your Worth

One reason self-worth suffers is mixing who you are with what you do. For example, if you make a mistake at work, you may think, "I am a failure." In reality, one mistake does not make you a failure as a person. It just means you messed up a task. Learning to see your actions as separate from your core worth can help you recover more smoothly from errors. It also keeps you from feeling shame every time you do not perform perfectly.

Here is a way to practice this:

1. **Notice the Thought**: "I failed at this task."
2. **Stay Objective**: "Yes, I did not complete that project well."
3. **Resist the Leap**: Do not jump to "I am worthless." Instead, say, "I am still a capable person who can learn from this."

This shift takes time, but it can stop you from sinking into negative self-talk that worsens anger.

---

## Building Self-Worth with Affirmations

Affirmations are short, positive statements you repeat to yourself. They can push back against the critical inner voice that tries to lower your value. Here are some examples:

- "I have strengths that matter."
- "I am allowed to make mistakes and grow."
- "My feelings are valid, including anger."
- "I can handle challenges without giving up on myself."

You can say them in the morning, before bed, or whenever you catch yourself thinking negatively. Affirmations are not magic words. They work over time, bit by bit, by replacing negative ideas with kinder ones.

---

## Setting and Achieving Small Goals

Nothing boosts confidence like seeing yourself succeed. When low self-worth holds you back, you might aim too high or too low. If you aim too high and fail, you might feel worse. If you aim too low, you never see what you are capable of. The answer is to set realistic, small goals that stretch you just enough:

1. **Pick One Area**
   Maybe you want to improve your speaking skills or manage your finances better. Choose one area rather than many at once.
2. **Define a Mini-Goal**
   For example, if public speaking scares you, a mini-goal might be to share

a small idea in a team meeting at work. If that still feels too big, break it down even more—maybe practice your idea aloud at home first.
3. **Take the Step**
Even if you are nervous, do your best to follow through.
4. **Acknowledge the Progress**
Recognize that you took action. Do not brush it off. Tell yourself, "I did something that felt challenging, and I survived it."

With each small success, your confidence can grow. You learn that you can face fears or tasks without falling apart, which helps you handle anger triggers more calmly.

---

## Learning to Trust Yourself

Low self-worth often goes hand in hand with a lack of trust in your own judgment. You might rely on others to make decisions for you, or you might second-guess every choice. This self-doubt can cause anger when you feel forced into situations you do not like, or when you feel you have no control. To grow self-trust:

- **Make a Simple Choice Each Day**
  It could be choosing what to wear, what to eat, or where to walk. Decide quickly and stick to it.
- **Accept Mistakes as Learning**
  If a choice does not go well, see it as a lesson, not proof that you are incompetent. Ask, "What can I learn?" rather than "Why am I so foolish?"
- **Listen to Your Gut**
  If something feels wrong to you, pause and consider why. It may be that your instincts are picking up on a problem.

As you trust yourself more, you might find you feel calmer in stressful situations, because you know you can rely on your own judgment.

---

## Handling Criticism with Confidence

Even confident people face criticism, but they do not let it crush their self-worth. They see critique as feedback on a specific action, not a verdict on who they are. Here is how you can handle criticism without rage or self-hate:

1. **Pause Before Responding**
   Take a breath. Is the person criticizing you in a useful way, or are they being rude? Try to figure out if there is truth in their words.
2. **Ask for Clarity**
   If the criticism seems unclear, ask politely, "Can you tell me more about what you think I should improve?" This shows you are open to learning.
3. **Agree or Disagree Calmly**
   If you feel the critique is valid, you can say, "Thank you, I see your point." If you disagree, you can say, "I understand your view, but here is my perspective."
4. **Avoid Personal Attacks**
   Focus on the issue, not on insulting the person who criticized you or turning anger inward.

With practice, you can take in criticism without letting it destroy your peace. You decide what is helpful and what is not. This balanced approach reduces anger flare-ups that can happen when you feel attacked.

---

## Surround Yourself with Positive People

Your environment can either nurture your confidence or wear it down. If you spend time with people who constantly belittle you, call you names, or dismiss your feelings, your self-worth can sink. If possible, aim to:

- **Seek Supportive Friends**: People who respect your feelings, cheer on your progress, and offer honest help when needed.
- **Limit Time with Toxic Individuals**: If someone makes you feel small or always criticizes you, see if you can reduce how much time you spend with them.
- **Join Groups That Encourage Growth**: This could be a local meetup related to a hobby, an online forum for people with similar interests, or a class that helps you learn new skills.

When you feel safe and valued in your environment, your anger is less likely to erupt from feeling constantly judged or cornered.

## Learning New Skills

Developing a new skill can boost self-worth because it shows you that you can grow and adapt. You might learn a language, pick up a craft, try coding, or explore any topic that excites you. The idea is to prove to yourself that you can start as a beginner and improve over time:

1. **Choose Something You Care About**
   If the skill does not interest you, you will not stay motivated.
2. **Accept Mistakes as Part of Learning**
   This helps you practice patience with yourself, which can spill over into patience when angry feelings rise.
3. **Track Progress**
   Keep a simple record of what you learn each week. Seeing how far you have come builds pride in your efforts.

As your sense of ability grows, you may feel more confident tackling life's challenges instead of responding with anger or hiding in self-doubt.

---

## Setting Personal Boundaries

You cannot raise confidence and self-worth if people constantly cross your limits. Learning to set personal boundaries tells others how you expect to be treated. It also tells yourself that you have value. Examples of boundaries include:

- **Time Boundaries**: "I need an hour of quiet after work before talking about big topics."
- **Emotional Boundaries**: "I will not respond to yelling. If you raise your voice, I will pause this conversation."
- **Physical Boundaries**: "I do not want hugs or touching without my permission."
- **Digital Boundaries**: "I do not answer work emails after 7 PM."

When you create and respect your own boundaries, you send a strong message to your mind that you deserve respect and care.

## Positive Body Language

Confidence also shows up in how you carry yourself. Standing or sitting with your shoulders back and your head held high can make you feel more self-assured, even if you do not feel it at first. Avoid slumping, crossing your arms tightly, or looking at the ground all the time. Small shifts like making eye contact when you speak can help you believe in yourself more, which can decrease feelings of anger that come from low self-confidence.

---

## Acknowledging Your Strengths

It is easy to focus on flaws, but you do have strengths. Maybe you are good at listening, or you keep a cool head in emergencies, or you have a knack for solving puzzles. Think of at least one positive quality you possess. This is not bragging; it is reminding yourself that you have good points. You can also ask a friend or family member what they admire in you. Write these down and look at them when you feel low. This practice can build self-worth by balancing negative thoughts.

---

## Handling Jealousy and Envy

Low self-worth can cause jealousy toward people who seem more confident or successful. That jealousy can turn into anger, either directed at them or at yourself. To manage envy:

1. **Admit the Feeling**
   "I am jealous because they have what I want."
2. **Ask What You Really Desire**
   Is it their job, their relationship, their free time, or their skill? Identifying it helps you see what you might work toward.
3. **Focus on Your Path**
   Instead of wishing you were them, ask yourself how you can move closer to your own goals.
4. **Wish Them Well**
   It might feel odd, but silently wishing others well can reduce envy. Realize that their success does not take away from your potential.

Turning envy into inspiration can raise your motivation instead of fueling angry comparisons.

## Seeing Anger As a Sign of Underlying Needs

When your self-worth is low, you might not notice your own needs until you are extremely upset. Anger can be a clue that something in your life is off balance—perhaps you feel disrespected, lonely, or undervalued. With a healthy sense of worth, you pick up on these needs earlier. You realize, "I deserve respect," and you speak up before anger explodes. You might say, "I need time alone right now," or "I do not like how you spoke to me," in a calm tone. This approach can prevent full-blown anger by addressing the problem sooner.

## Overcoming the Fear of Judgment

If you have low self-worth, you might fear that others are judging you whenever you speak or act. This fear can paralyze you. Then, when you do speak up, it might come out as anger because you are so tense. Building confidence means understanding that people's opinions do not define you. Some might like what you do; some might not. That is normal. If you are acting in line with your values, that is what counts. You do not have to be perfect to be worthwhile.

## Affirming Your Right to Be Heard

A core part of self-worth is believing that your voice matters. This does not mean always demanding attention. It means recognizing that you have a viewpoint worth sharing. If you find that you never talk in meetings or always let others decide things at home, try small steps:

- **Speak Up Once**: Decide you will share at least one idea at the next meeting or family discussion.
- **Express a Preference**: If your friend asks where you want to eat, name a place you like. This might feel small, but it is practice in showing that your choices matter.

Each time you allow yourself to be heard, you reinforce the idea that you count, which can reduce the anger that comes from feeling invisible.

## Acknowledging Each Step Forward

Raising confidence and self-worth takes patience. Each small victory—finishing a project, speaking up when you would have stayed silent, or noticing a negative thought and changing it—deserves your recognition. These steps might feel tiny in the moment, but they add up to big change over time. By noticing each bit of progress, you strengthen your resolve to keep going. This also lowers frustration, because you see that you are moving ahead rather than staying stuck.

## When to Seek Help for Low Self-Worth

Sometimes low self-worth runs deep, possibly linked to past trauma, bullying, or a childhood where you were often criticized. If you find that self-help methods are not improving your view of yourself, or if you feel constant shame, it might be best to talk to a counselor or join a support group. Professional guidance can help uncover hidden beliefs that keep you feeling small. It can also teach you new ways to see your strengths and cope with life's demands. Reaching out for help does not mean you have failed; it means you are taking a step to care for yourself.

## Tying It All Together

Confidence and self-worth work like a shield against unhealthy anger. When you see your own value, you can be honest about your feelings without fear that they make you a bad person. You can set boundaries, say "no" when needed, and express frustration calmly instead of feeling trapped or powerless. You can also handle criticism or setbacks without concluding that you are worthless.

# Chapter 13: Dealing with Anger in the Workplace

Anger at work can be a tough challenge. You might feel pressured by deadlines, overloaded by responsibilities, or upset with how a coworker or manager treats you. In some workplaces, employees feel like they do not have a voice, or that they must constantly prove their worth to stay employed. These conditions can light a fuse that causes anger to flare. In this chapter, we will look at common sources of anger in the workplace, what happens when anger is not handled well, and specific methods to manage that anger in a healthy way. By learning to address anger at work, you can protect your own well-being and build stronger, more professional relationships with colleagues.

---

## Recognizing Sources of Workplace Anger

It helps to identify what triggers your anger on the job. You might see one or more of the following factors:

1. **Unfair Treatment**
   Maybe your boss gives a coworker easier tasks while you receive the hardest ones. Or perhaps your ideas are often ignored during meetings. Feelings of unfairness or favoritism can stir resentment.
2. **Excessive Workload**
   Many employees feel angry when the tasks and hours required surpass what they can handle. Working late nights or rushing to meet tight deadlines can lead to frustration and burnout.
3. **Poor Communication**
   Misunderstandings can grow if messages are not clear, or if colleagues fail to share important details in a timely manner. When people are kept in the dark, they may feel disrespected or left out.
4. **Conflict with Coworkers**
   Clashing personalities, power struggles, or differences in work styles can lead to tension. Even minor issues, like a colleague who always arrives late or speaks in a rude tone, can cause ongoing annoyance.
5. **Inadequate Pay or Benefits**
   If you believe your compensation is too low for the effort you invest, you

may feel resentful. Anger can emerge when you sense that your hard work is under-valued.

6. **Harassment or Bullying**
   If someone at work consistently disrespects you, makes mean remarks, or tries to sabotage you, your anger may rise. This behavior can create a toxic environment and should not be overlooked.

Each workplace is unique. By pinpointing specific triggers, you can focus on realistic strategies to address them rather than letting frustration build.

---

## Negative Results of Mismanaged Workplace Anger

When anger stays unaddressed at work, it can lead to problems not only for the individual but for the entire team or company:

1. **Reduced Productivity**
   An angry mind has difficulty focusing. You might spend more time stewing over what upset you than completing your tasks.
2. **Damaged Relationships**
   Yelling or lashing out at colleagues can break trust. You might also notice coworkers avoiding you, which hurts teamwork and communication.
3. **Low Workplace Morale**
   If anger spreads among employees, the entire environment can become gloomy. People might dread coming to work or avoid group projects.
4. **Increased Errors**
   Working in a constant state of agitation can lead to poor judgment and rushed decisions, causing mistakes in important tasks.
5. **Health Problems**
   Chronic anger and stress at work can lead to headaches, digestion problems, and trouble sleeping. This can weaken your overall health.
6. **Reputation Damage**
   If people see you as someone who flies off the handle, it may harm your professional standing. Promotions or new opportunities might pass you by if management worries about your temper.

Learning to manage workplace anger is not just about feeling better—it is also about securing your position, maintaining productive relationships, and ensuring you can perform at your best.

## Taking Charge of Your Own Behavior

You may not be able to change all the workplace factors that upset you, such as a tight deadline or a rude colleague, but you can control how you respond. Taking responsibility for your own reactions is a key step in managing anger at work.

1. **Identify Your Warning Signs**
   Notice how your body feels when anger starts to build. Do you feel your stomach clench? Does your jaw tighten? Recognizing these early signs can help you step away or cool down before you lose your temper.
2. **Pause and Breathe**
   A brief pause can stop you from saying something you will regret. Take a few slow breaths, count to three, or take a quick sip of water. This small break can reset your mind so you can respond more calmly.
3. **Use Private Outlets for Immediate Anger**
   If you feel you might snap, excuse yourself to the restroom or a quiet area. You can take several deep breaths, silently talk yourself down, or jot a few notes on a piece of paper about what is upsetting you. Let that initial surge pass before returning to the main area.
4. **Pick Your Battles**
   Not every frustration deserves a confrontation. Ask yourself, "Is this issue important enough to address, or can I let it go?" Sometimes, ignoring minor irritations helps preserve your energy for real problems.
5. **Avoid Triangular Conflict**
   This is when you involve a third person in your dispute rather than speaking directly to the person who upset you. Spreading complaints around the office can cause gossip and widen the conflict. If possible, communicate directly with the person involved, or seek a manager or HR rep if it involves harassment or deeper issues.

Taking charge of your own reactions shows maturity and signals to others that you want to keep the workplace functional. It does not mean you ignore serious problems, but it does mean you handle them with a calm approach.

## Communicating Anger Without Burning Bridges

When an issue at work truly needs attention, you have a right to raise it. The key is doing so without letting anger overshadow the real problem. These steps can help:

1. **Plan Your Words**
   Before you meet or send an email about the issue, outline what you want to say. Keep it factual. For example, instead of, "You never help me," you might say, "I've noticed I'm handling five assignments, while you have one. Can we find a better balance?"
2. **Mind Your Tone**
   Aim for calm and level communication. If you find your voice getting louder, pause, breathe, and try again. Yelling or using harsh words can make the other person defensive.
3. **Use "I" Statements**
   Similar to what we discussed in earlier chapters, phrases like "I feel frustrated when ___" or "I need more clarity on ___" focus on your experience rather than assigning blame.
4. **Offer Possible Solutions**
   Rather than just complaining, propose something workable. "I would appreciate a schedule that divides tasks more evenly," or "Can we set aside ten minutes each morning to discuss any urgent updates?" This shows you want to fix the situation, not just rant.
5. **Agree on Next Steps**
   If you talk to a coworker or manager about a problem, see if you can agree on clear steps. For instance, "We will both try this new approach for a week and revisit how it's going next Monday." Setting a timeline can prevent misunderstandings later.

Communicating anger in this measured way does not mean you are weak. On the contrary, it shows professionalism, respect, and a willingness to solve problems rather than fan the flames.

## Handling Difficult People and Situations

Some workplace anger stems from situations or individuals who are consistently challenging. For instance, you might deal with a manager who yells often or a coworker who constantly criticizes you. Here are some ideas for these cases:

1. **Stay Grounded in Facts**
   When someone is abrasive, it can trigger emotional reactions. Focus on the facts of the situation. If your manager is upset because of a missed deadline, discuss the timeline and tasks instead of being pulled into personal attacks.
2. **Protect Your Time**
   If a difficult colleague takes up too much of your time with complaints or negativity, politely limit your interactions. For example, you could say, "I have to get back to my project, so I only have five minutes to talk."
3. **Practice Calm Repetition**
   If someone is pushing you in a conversation, you can calmly repeat your stance: "I understand you're upset, but I need the information emailed to me. Let's revisit this once I receive it." Repeating the statement, without raising your voice, can hold your boundary.
4. **Document Problematic Behavior**
   If you suspect you might need evidence later—especially for harassment or bullying—keep a simple record of dates, times, and what happened. This can be important if you need to speak to HR or higher management.
5. **Know When to Escalate**
   If the behavior is discriminatory, threatening, or harmful to your mental health, go to HR or a supervisor. Do not feel you must handle serious issues alone. Seek professional support within your organization or from an outside counselor if needed.

These approaches can help protect you and reduce constant tension. Some difficult workplace relationships may improve over time if you remain calm and consistent, though not every situation will fully resolve.

---

## Balancing Personal Feelings with Professionalism

You might have days when personal stress spills into your job. Perhaps you are dealing with family issues, financial troubles, or health concerns. Anger you feel from these challenges can show up in your responses to coworkers or tasks. While it is normal for personal and work lives to overlap at times, you can find ways to lessen the impact of outside stress on your workplace attitude:

1. **Set a Mental Transition**
   Before starting your shift or opening your laptop, take a brief moment to remind yourself that you are stepping into work. You might say silently, "I will focus on my job for the next eight hours, and set my personal worries aside if I can."
2. **Use Breaks Wisely**
   If personal feelings are overwhelming, step outside for fresh air or a short walk. Use these minutes to manage your emotions instead of lashing out at a colleague.
3. **Avoid Oversharing**
   While it can help to have a close work friend who understands your personal stress, be mindful about sharing details with many coworkers. If you regret telling private stories, that added stress could increase feelings of shame or frustration.
4. **Seek Support Outside of Work**
   A counselor or a trusted friend away from the office might help you process personal problems. That way, you are less likely to bring unresolved issues into the workplace each day.

When you see a coworker struggling because of outside stress, you might offer a kind word or brief help. However, remember you are not responsible for solving their problems. Encouraging them to seek proper help is often more useful than taking on their burdens yourself.

---

## Managing Stress and Anger on Remote Teams

These days, many people work remotely, either partially or fully. Remote work can reduce in-person conflicts, but it can also cause stress or anger in other ways:

1. **Tech Glitches**
   Slow internet, software errors, or connectivity problems can be frustrating. When these issues happen during a big deadline or meeting, anger can rise quickly.

2. **Blurry Boundaries**
   Working from home can blur the line between personal time and job tasks. You might feel like you never fully log off. This can lead to irritability.
3. **Lack of Face-to-Face Cues**
   In virtual meetings, you cannot see everyone's body language clearly. Misunderstandings are easier if someone's tone or facial expressions are lost on camera.
4. **Feelings of Isolation**
   Remote workers might miss the friendly chats that happen in an office, which can lead to loneliness or frustration, making them more prone to anger or outbursts during virtual calls.

To manage these challenges:

- **Create a Workspace**: Even if it is a small corner, having a dedicated spot for your computer can help you mentally separate work from personal life.
- **Set Work Hours**: If possible, decide when you start and stop each day. Try to protect your personal time from constant messages and emails.
- **Double-Check Tone**: In emails and chat messages, read over what you wrote to ensure it is calm and clear, not fueled by anger or sarcasm.
- **Speak Up Promptly**: If you sense a misunderstanding in a remote setting, address it early. A short phone call or video chat can clear the air faster than a string of emails.

By staying proactive about these remote work issues, you can prevent small annoyances from escalating into big anger problems.

---

## Keeping Perspective on Workplace Problems

Sometimes anger takes over when a single work issue feels huge. You might feel as though everything hinges on one project or disagreement. While your job is important, try to keep a wider view:

- **Remember It Is Not Permanent**: Jobs and roles can change. Even if you are dealing with a difficult boss now, the future may bring a new boss or a new position.

- **Look for Small Wins**: Even if the overall environment is tough, notice small positives, like finishing a complex task or helping a coworker succeed.
- **Seek Growth Opportunities**: A challenging workplace can teach you skills in conflict resolution, communication, and stress management that could help you in future roles.
- **Stay Open to Other Options**: If the environment is truly harming your well-being, consider looking for a different job. You are not trapped, though changing jobs may require planning and effort.

Maintaining perspective can prevent anger from clouding your entire mindset. It also helps you decide whether to stay and improve your situation or move on to something healthier.

---

## Tips for Leaders and Managers

If you manage a team, you can help reduce anger at work by fostering a supportive environment:

1. **Set Clear Expectations**
   Make sure everyone understands roles, deadlines, and procedures. Confusion can spark frustration.
2. **Listen Actively**
   Invite employees to share concerns without fear of punishment. Hearing them out can resolve small issues before they become big problems.
3. **Encourage Balance**
   If your team is overloaded, see if tasks can be shifted or if deadlines can be adjusted. Overworked employees tend to be more irritable.
4. **Provide Feedback Kindly**
   When correcting someone's work, focus on the task rather than attacking their character. Simple tips can prevent defensive anger.
5. **Model Calm Behavior**
   As a leader, your actions set the tone. If you handle setbacks or stress with composure, employees may follow suit. If you are prone to yelling, they might believe that is acceptable.

Leaders who value emotional well-being in the workplace can shape a culture where anger is addressed early and constructively, rather than spreading through the team.

## Taking Breaks and Holidays Seriously

Some workplaces build a culture where employees feel guilty for taking time off or stepping away from their desks. This can feed resentment and anger over time. Rest is important for emotional balance:

- **Use Vacation Days**: If you have days off or personal leave, plan to use them. Time away can refresh your mind and help you return in a calmer state.
- **Encourage Your Colleagues to Rest**: If you manage or mentor others, remind them to take breaks when needed. A well-rested team tends to be less stressed.
- **Plan Small Recharge Moments**: Even if you cannot take a long trip, you might arrange a day where you do something relaxing, such as reading or going for a slow walk.

Allowing yourself rest can prevent build-up of frustration that leads to anger. When you feel less resentful about your workload or schedule, you are more likely to respond thoughtfully to problems that arise.

## Seeking Support If Work Anger Feels Overwhelming

If anger at work causes you deep distress, or if you find yourself raging frequently, consider talking to a professional. A counselor or therapist can help you uncover underlying causes, such as past experiences or personal triggers that flare at work. Sometimes, short-term therapy focusing on workplace stress can provide new tactics for communication, boundary-setting, and relaxation.

You can also reach out to a friend or family member just to talk things through. Sometimes describing the conflict aloud helps you see a solution you missed before. If a coworker is also feeling frustrated, you could share strategies and support each other in handling stress more constructively. However, be cautious about turning these talks into gripe sessions that only fuel anger further. Aim for a balance of venting and problem-solving.

## Checking Your Personal Role

It is worth asking if any of your own actions might worsen the anger climate at work. For example, do you sometimes complain a lot or make sarcastic remarks to coworkers? Do you hold onto small grudges and bring them up repeatedly? Be honest with yourself. Recognizing your part in the cycle can be humbling, but it is an important step toward a healthier environment.

If you realize that you have contributed to tension, take ownership. You might speak privately with a colleague you have argued with and say, "I realize I have not always been patient. I would like us to move forward with more respect." Apologizing sincerely, if it fits the situation, can defuse built-up anger on both sides.

## Building Positive Relationships at Work

Constructive, friendly relationships can buffer against anger when problems arise. Even if you do not become best friends with your coworkers, showing basic goodwill can help. You might:

- **Greet People by Name**: A quick "Hello, how are you?" can start the day on a positive note.
- **Show Genuine Interest**: Ask about their weekend or an interest they have. Just be sure not to pry if they do not seem comfortable.
- **Offer Help Occasionally**: If you have a few minutes, you might say, "Do you need a hand with that?" This fosters mutual support.
- **Give Small Thanks**: A simple "Thank you for clarifying that," or "I appreciate your input," can go a long way toward building a sense of teamwork.

When you have a few allies at work, you might feel less alone in handling stress or speaking up about issues. This support network can ease anger because you know you have someone to talk to or stand by you if a conflict arises.

# Chapter 14: Helping Family and Friends Understand

Anger can be a very private emotion, but it affects the people closest to you—your family, friends, and others you see often. When they do not know what is going on inside your mind, they may misunderstand your anger, feel hurt by it, or worry that they caused it. On the other hand, if you have supportive people in your life who understand your triggers and are willing to help, you can find better ways to handle anger together. In this chapter, we will look at why it is important to help your loved ones understand your anger, along with practical steps you can take to explain your feelings, set boundaries, and ask for their support without pushing them away.

---

## Why Involving Loved Ones Matters

Some individuals prefer to solve their anger problems quietly. They might feel embarrassed to let others see that they struggle with frustration or outbursts. However, loved ones are often the first to notice when you are stressed, and their reactions can either calm you or make the anger worse. Sharing information about your anger:

1. **Lessens Confusion**
   If you occasionally snap at a friend for no obvious reason, they might think you do not care about them. Explaining that you are dealing with intense anger or stress can clear up their confusion.
2. **Builds a Team Effort**
   Family and friends can offer help if they understand what you are facing. They might give you space when you show signs of building frustration, or they could remind you of calming strategies you have chosen to use.
3. **Prevents Misinformation**
   Without an explanation, people might guess at the reasons behind your anger. They could assume you are upset with them personally or interpret your mood in the wrong way.
4. **Helps You Stay Accountable**
   When people around you know you are working on handling anger better,

they can gently call attention to moments when you slip back into old habits. This can keep you on track.

By involving loved ones, you shift from battling anger alone to having a circle of support. You do not have to share every detail, but open communication can help them see the larger picture and respond in ways that foster peace rather than more tension.

---

## Explaining Your Anger in Simple Terms

Talking about anger can feel awkward or risky if you fear judgment. Still, a clear explanation can reduce misunderstandings. Here are some tips for discussing it with someone you trust:

1. **Choose a Calm Moment**
   It is best to talk about anger when you are not angry. Pick a time when you both feel relaxed. Mention that you have something important to discuss and ask if this is a good time for them to listen.
2. **Describe What Happens Internally**
   Let them know the physical or mental signs you experience. For example, "My heart races, and I feel like I cannot think straight." This helps them see that anger is not just a mood you turn on and off.
3. **Share Triggers**
   If you have noticed certain triggers—such as feeling criticized at work, being overtired, or dealing with a messy environment—tell them. Stress that it is not their fault if these triggers occur, but that knowing about them can help prevent flare-ups.
4. **Explain How They Can Help**
   Many people want to help but do not know how. You might say, "When I seem tense, it helps if you speak softly," or "If I start getting agitated, reminding me to take a short walk can calm me." Giving them direct ideas helps them feel useful rather than helpless.
5. **Thank Them for Listening**
   Showing appreciation can build a sense of teamwork. It also encourages them to keep supporting you rather than feeling burdened.

This kind of conversation might feel strange at first, but it lays the foundation for better mutual understanding. If the person seems confused or uncertain, invite them to ask questions. Make it clear you value their presence in your life.

---

## Correcting Myths About Anger

Friends or family might hold certain beliefs about anger that can block real help. Some myths include:

- **"Anger is always bad."**
  Your loved ones might worry that if you admit you are angry, it means you are doing something wrong. Let them know anger is a normal emotion that signals a problem.
- **"Just smile and move on."**
  Some might think you can fix anger by ignoring it. Explain that holding it in can lead to bigger outbursts later.
- **"If you are angry, it must be someone else's fault."**
  Your friends might blame themselves or think they did something to cause your anger. Remind them that anger can arise from many sources, not just personal conflicts.
- **"Anger is dangerous."**
  People might fear that anger always leads to aggression. You can share that you are learning safe ways to express it, so it does not become harmful.

When you clarify these points, you reduce the chance of loved ones reacting with fear or confusion. They may be more open to helping you manage anger once they realize it is not a moral failing or a sign that you despise them.

---

## Asking for Understanding and Not Control

You want your loved ones to understand your anger, but they cannot fix it for you. It is important to avoid placing the responsibility for your feelings on them. For instance, you might say:

- "I want you to know that sometimes I get upset because of high stress. If I look tense or raise my voice, please know it's not always directed at you."
- "It helps me when you give me a moment to cool down, rather than pressing me to talk immediately."

These statements invite their support but do not demand that they walk on eggshells around you or handle your emotions for you. You are still responsible for your actions and reactions.

If a loved one tries to take charge, such as constantly asking, "Are you angry now? Should I back off?" you can kindly set a boundary: "I appreciate your concern, but it is also important that I learn to recognize my own anger signals. Let's agree that if I really need your help, I will let you know."

---

## Handling Loved Ones Who Dismiss Your Anger

Not everyone will be understanding. Some family members or friends might say things like, "You're overreacting," or "You should just toughen up." This can worsen your anger if you feel dismissed. Here are ways to respond:

1. **Stay Firm in Your Feelings**
   "I hear what you are saying, but I know my anger is real. I am working on it in a healthy way."
2. **Offer Brief Explanations**
   Repeat a calm summary: "I feel stress building up. I am trying to manage it. I would appreciate if you do not make light of it."
3. **Limit Deep Talks**
   If they continue to dismiss you, consider spending less time discussing your anger with them. Focus on people who respect your feelings.
4. **Look for Patterns**
   If someone always trivializes your emotions, you might realize you cannot rely on that person for emotional support. Knowing this can help you adjust your expectations and avoid repeated disappointment.

You cannot force others to respect your anger issues, but you can protect yourself from their dismissive attitudes. Focus on those who genuinely want to understand.

## Teaching Loved Ones Basic De-escalation Tips

When you do get angry at home or among friends, it helps if people around you know simple ways to avoid making it worse. You might suggest they try:

1. **Staying Calm**
   If they yell back or speak sarcastically, it can fuel your anger. A quieter tone helps defuse the heat.
2. **Respecting Personal Space**
   Standing too close or blocking your exit can make you feel trapped. Keeping a bit of distance can help you breathe more freely.
3. **Using Gentle Reminders**
   If you have agreed on a calming word or phrase, hearing it might remind you to pause before you say something hurtful.
4. **Allowing Time**
   Pressuring you to resolve things instantly can push your anger higher. A short break can be more productive than forcing a conversation at the peak of your frustration.

Make it clear that you are not asking them to manage or "fix" you. You only want them to avoid behaviors that pour more fuel on the fire. This knowledge can help loved ones feel more confident in tense moments.

---

## Sharing Tools and Methods You Are Practicing

If you have been learning certain methods to handle anger—like deep breathing, writing down your thoughts, or taking a quick walk—tell the people close to you about these. They can gently remind you to use them or help set up the conditions for these methods to work. For example, if you find that playing soft music helps you calm down, a family member might turn on that playlist when they see you growing upset. Or if a friend notices you usually step into another room to breathe, they might offer to watch the kids for a few minutes so you can do so.

By talking about your chosen strategies, you transform your family or friends into supporters of those positive habits. It also shows them you are serious about managing your anger, which can build trust in your efforts.

## Encouraging Empathy in Both Directions

It is easy to focus on how you want others to understand your anger, but empathy goes both ways. Consider the feelings of those who see you angry:

- **They May Worry About You**
  A spouse or friend might feel helpless when you are upset and wonder if they did something wrong.
- **They May Fear Conflict**
  Some people grew up in homes where anger led to hurtful actions. Seeing a loved one angry might trigger their own anxiety or memories.
- **They May Feel Blamed**
  If your anger shows up a lot, they might assume they are failing to support you correctly.

Try to see their viewpoint. You can reassure them that you care about their comfort and do not wish to scare or blame them. By acknowledging their feelings, you show you respect their well-being too, which can create a stronger bond.

---

## Avoiding Manipulation

Sometimes, people use anger to get their way with loved ones. They might raise their voice to push others into giving in or threaten to withdraw affection unless the other person agrees with them. This is not healthy anger expression—it is manipulation. If you catch yourself doing this, take a step back:

- **Own Your Behavior**
  Admit you are using anger to control or intimidate. It can be painful to realize, but honesty is necessary for change.
- **Apologize**
  If you have manipulated a friend or family member through anger, a clear apology can help rebuild trust. "I realize I was using my anger to force a decision, and that wasn't right."
- **Set a Plan to Stop**
  Decide on a strategy, like pausing conversations if you notice yourself pressuring the other person. Communicate that strategy openly.

Healthy support from loved ones only happens when anger is not used as a tool to dominate them. Recognizing any manipulative habits is an essential step in building mutual respect.

## When Loved Ones Trigger Your Anger Often

It can be trickier if the people closest to you are also major sources of your anger. You might have a relative who criticizes you non-stop or a friend who teases you about sensitive topics. Here are some approaches:

1. **Set Boundaries**
   Explain calmly which topics are off-limits, or let them know that constant criticism harms your relationship. If they refuse to respect that boundary, you may need to reduce time with them.
2. **Choose When to Engage**
   If you know a certain family gathering always ends in arguments, decide whether you want to attend. If you do go, plan a short visit or have a backup plan to leave early if anger starts to build.
3. **Use a Friend as Support**
   Take a supportive friend or partner to family events. They can help you stay calm or remind you to step away if tension rises.
4. **Seek Mediation**
   If the conflict is severe (such as with a parent or sibling), a mediator or counselor might help you both communicate better, reducing triggers that lead to anger.

You might not be able to change their behavior, but you can protect your emotional health by setting limits on how much negative treatment you will accept.

## Helping Children Understand Adult Anger

If you have children, they may see you angry at times. Children often blame themselves if a parent or guardian is upset. It is important to communicate with them in a way they can grasp:

1. **Use Simple Explanations**
   Say something like, "Mom feels tense because of her job, but I still love you. I'm not mad at you." Keep it short and clear.
2. **Apologize When Needed**
   If you yell at a child in frustration, let them know you are sorry. This models healthy communication and shows them that even grown-ups make mistakes.
3. **Teach Them About Emotions**
   You can say, "Everyone feels anger sometimes. It's okay to feel angry, but let's learn good ways to handle it." Show them simple calming techniques they can try as well.
4. **Assure Them of Safety**
   Children need to know your anger will not harm them. If you do lose your temper, reassure them afterward that they are safe, and you are working on controlling your emotions.

By being open about anger, you can break cycles where children learn to fear or replicate outbursts they see at home. Instead, they can grow up understanding that anger can be managed without harming anyone.

---

## Cultural or Generational Differences

In some cultures, anger is more accepted as a normal part of expression. In others, it is heavily frowned upon. Older family members might believe in keeping emotions hidden, while younger relatives might be more open about sharing feelings. If you are in a mixed setting, misunderstandings about anger can multiply. You can:

- **Clarify Your Perspective**
  Let older relatives know that you are not trying to disrespect traditions; you simply want to handle your anger in a healthier way that includes talking about it.
- **Show Respect for Their Views**
  If they prefer more privacy around emotions, do not force them to have long talks. Instead, adapt how you ask for their support.
- **Use Patience**
  Cultural and generational differences do not change overnight. Keep

communication calm and consistent, and try to see where they are coming from.

Over time, they might become more comfortable with open discussions if they see it helps you stay calmer and happier.

---

## Protecting Your Own Boundaries

Though you want family and friends to understand your anger, you have a right to privacy and personal space. If someone pushes too much or attempts to pry into your personal reasons for feeling upset, you can say:

- **"I appreciate your concern, but this is all I'm comfortable sharing right now."**
- **"I'm still working through this. I'll let you know if I need to talk more."**

Setting limits with well-meaning loved ones does not mean you are ungrateful. It simply means you need time to process your emotions in a way that feels safe.

---

## Recognizing When Outside Help Is Needed

If your anger has led to severe conflicts within your family or circle of friends—such as constant fights, isolation, or even threats of harm—it may be time to involve a professional. Family therapy or counseling can guide everyone toward better communication. A counselor can help each person see their role in conflicts and learn new methods to avoid power struggles. Bringing an unbiased third party into these discussions can reduce blame and help people focus on solutions. Even a few sessions can open new paths for understanding.

---

## Strengthening Bonds Through Shared Effort

Involving family and friends in your anger management efforts can deepen your relationships. You might:

- **Hold Small Check-Ins**: Once in a while, ask each other, "How are we doing with communication? Anything we can do better?"
- **Praise Helpful Actions**: If someone respects a boundary you set or gives you the space you requested, thank them. Likewise, you can appreciate their honesty if they mention a concern in a calm way.
- **Stay Open to Their Input**: Sometimes loved ones see patterns you do not. Even if their feedback stings, consider whether there is truth in it.

This approach can turn anger management into something that strengthens family unity, rather than tearing it apart. People may feel relieved to know they can help, and you may find more patience for yourself when you see others acknowledging your efforts.

---

# Chapter 15: Changing Negative Thoughts into Positive Ones

Negative thoughts can make anger stronger. If you often think the worst about yourself, other people, or situations, you may feel edgy and ready to snap. But if you learn to recognize negative thoughts and switch them to more balanced thinking, you can lower your anger levels. In this chapter, we will look at why negative thoughts fuel anger, how to notice them in your mind, and ways to shift them toward more positive or fair perspectives. With practice, you can help your mind become a calmer place, which reduces the chance of boiling anger.

---

## Why Negative Thoughts Fuel Anger

When your mind is full of unhelpful ideas, you might jump to harsh conclusions or assume others mean you harm. These thoughts can make you feel targeted or hopeless, and anger often follows. Some ways negative thoughts feed anger include:

1. **Seeing Threats Everywhere**
   If your mind constantly says, "People are out to get me," you might overreact to small slights. You could take a simple comment from a friend as a personal attack.
2. **Unfair Self-Criticism**
   When you keep telling yourself, "I am a failure," you might feel frustrated and hopeless. Anger can come from being harsh on yourself because you never feel at ease inside.
3. **Expecting the Worst**
   Believing that everything will turn out badly creates tension. You stay on edge, bracing for failure or conflict, which makes anger more likely when even small problems arise.
4. **Blaming Others Automatically**
   If your default view is "It is always their fault," you might ignore your own role in conflicts. This can spark anger at people around you without stopping to see the bigger picture.

Negative thoughts are not always obvious. They can pass quickly through your mind, shaping your mood before you even notice them. That is why building awareness is a key first step to change.

---

## Identifying Common Negative Thinking Patterns

Many negative thoughts follow certain patterns. By spotting these patterns, you can catch them before they trigger anger. Some common ones include:

1. **All-or-Nothing Thinking**
   Seeing things in extremes: "If I am not the best, I am the worst." Or "If this plan fails, everything is ruined." This can create panic or despair that fuels anger.
2. **Overgeneralizing**
   Using words like "always" and "never" in your mind: "They never listen to me," or "I always mess up." This skips over the truth that life usually has shades of gray.
3. **Mind Reading**
   Assuming you know someone's thoughts or motives without proof: "She did that to hurt me," or "They are only being polite to hide how they really feel." This can spark anger based on guesses rather than facts.
4. **Fortune Telling**
   Predicting the worst: "I will fail for sure," or "They will laugh at me." These dark predictions can leave you feeling hopeless or angry.
5. **Labeling**
   Placing a harsh label on yourself or others: "I am an idiot," "He is a jerk," "She is useless." These labels block a fair view of what is really happening, causing more frustration.
6. **Discounting Positives**
   Ignoring good feedback or achievements: "Sure, they said I did well, but they are just being nice." This keeps you stuck in a negative bubble, fueling anger when stress hits.

By learning to spot these patterns, you can pause and see if your thoughts are accurate. This pause can help prevent an angry burst that stems from skewed thinking.

## The Thought-Emotion Link

Emotions like anger do not come out of thin air. They are often tied to what you say to yourself. Imagine two people stuck in traffic:

- Person A thinks: "I cannot believe how careless these drivers are. They are out to slow me down. This is ridiculous."
  This person might build anger quickly.
- Person B thinks: "Traffic is bad today, but it will pass. I will get there a bit late, but it is not the end of the world."
  This person might stay calmer.

The event (traffic) is the same. The difference is how each person's thoughts shape the emotion that follows. Once you see this link, you realize you have more control over anger than you might think. Changing thoughts does not mean ignoring real problems, but it lets you handle them with less rage and more clarity.

---

## Pausing to Catch Negative Thoughts

Before you can change a negative thought, you have to notice it. This is not always easy if you are used to letting your mind run on autopilot. Here are ways to improve awareness:

1. **Thought Journaling**
   Set aside a few minutes daily to write down situations that made you angry. Under each situation, jot the thoughts you remember having. Look for patterns or repeated ideas. Over time, you might see that you always think "no one values me" or "I am a mess" when you get upset.
2. **Check-Ins During the Day**
   Pause at different points—morning, lunch, evening—and ask yourself, "What is on my mind? How am I feeling?" If you are tense or angry, try to spot the thought that might be feeding that feeling.
3. **Physical Clues**
   Your body can warn you that negative thoughts are swirling. Tight shoulders, a clenched jaw, or a racing heart might suggest stress. When you notice these signs, ask yourself, "What am I telling myself right now?" You could be in a negative loop without realizing it.

Catching the thought early is often enough to reduce its power. Once you see it, you can decide if it is valid or needs adjusting.

---

## Challenging Negative Thoughts

After you notice a negative thought, the next step is to question it. Ask yourself:

1. **Is This Thought Completely True?**
   Look for evidence. If your mind says, "I always fail," think: "Have I truly failed at everything?" You might remember times you handled situations well.
2. **Am I Jumping to Conclusions?**
   If you are assuming someone dislikes you, do you have solid proof? Could there be another reason for their behavior?
3. **Is There a More Fair Way to See This?**
   Instead of "They are trying to make me look bad," a fairer thought might be, "They have not responded yet—I should ask for clarity."
4. **What Would I Tell a Friend in This Situation?**
   Often, we give friends balanced advice but treat ourselves harshly. Imagining a friend in your situation can help you see a more kind or realistic angle.

This is not about forcing fake positivity. It is about stepping back and checking if your thought matches reality. If you see that your thought is not entirely correct, you can replace it with one that better fits the facts.

---

## Replacing Negative Thoughts with Balanced Ones

Once you challenge a thought, you can rewrite it in your mind. For example:

- **Negative Thought**: "I am worthless at my job. My boss must hate me."
- **Balanced Thought**: "I made a mistake this week, but I have also done plenty of good work in the past. My boss might be disappointed, but that does not mean they hate me."

Notice that the replacement thought is not an over-the-top statement like, "I am perfect and beloved by everyone." Instead, it is realistic. Over time, practicing these balanced thoughts can reduce the anger that might come from harsh self-judgment or fear of others' opinions.

---

## Using Compassion with Yourself and Others

Negative thoughts often lack compassion. They may slam you for not being good enough or assume others are acting out of malice. Shifting to a gentle viewpoint can help:

1. **Self-Compassion**
   When you slip up, speak to yourself kindly. Rather than, "I am so stupid," say, "I made a mistake, but I can fix it or learn from it."
2. **Assume Good Intent**
   Instead of thinking, "They are trying to annoy me," consider, "Maybe they are having a tough day or do not realize they upset me." This does not excuse bad behavior, but it can stop anger from growing.
3. **Accept Flaws**
   Everyone is imperfect, including you. Recognizing that mistakes happen can ease the pressure. You can address problems without labeling yourself or others as completely bad.

Compassion does not mean letting people walk all over you. It just means you leave room for understanding before jumping to angry conclusions.

---

## Thought-Stopping Methods

Sometimes negative thoughts spin in your head repeatedly, making you more frustrated. A few techniques can break the loop:

1. **Visual Stop Sign**
   Imagine a big red STOP sign in your mind when negative thoughts start to race. This is a cue to shift your focus or talk back to the thought.
2. **Distraction**
   Move your attention to something else—count objects in the room, do a quick puzzle, or focus on a physical task. Even a short break can halt the cycle.

3. **Change Your Surroundings**
   If possible, leave the room where you are stuck in negative thinking. A new view can help your mind reset.

These methods are like pressing pause. After you stop the negative spiral, you can decide on a more balanced viewpoint.

---

## Positive Self-Talk

Replacing negative thoughts is easier if you have positive self-talk ready. This is not about telling yourself things that are untrue. It is about reminding yourself of strengths, past successes, and hopeful perspectives. Examples:

- "I can handle this, even if it is tough."
- "I have solved problems like this before."
- "I do not need to be perfect to be worthy."
- "Others' opinions do not define me."

You can write these on small notes to keep in a wallet or phone. Whenever you sense negativity, read one to shift your mental tone.

---

## Practicing Gratitude

A mind that never sees the good can get trapped in anger. Practicing gratitude helps you notice positives. Some simple ways:

1. **Daily Gratitude Listing**
   Each day, list a few things (big or small) you are thankful for—like a cozy bed or a supportive friend. This trains your brain to spot good aspects of life, which balances negativity.
2. **Thank People**
   If someone helps you or does something kind, thank them. Even a short message of thanks can warm your feelings and reduce frustration.
3. **Appreciate Small Moments**
   Pay attention to small joys—like the warmth of the sun or a pleasant taste of your favorite food. Let yourself feel it instead of rushing by.

This does not mean ignoring real problems. It just stops your mind from focusing only on what is wrong.

## Handling Doubt About Changing Thoughts

You might worry that trying to think in a more positive or balanced way is "lying to yourself" or "pretending everything is okay." But shifting negative thoughts does not deny problems. Instead, it:

- **Encourages a Fair View**: You can admit that something is stressful without believing it is hopeless.
- **Allows Growth**: You see mistakes as chances to improve, not final evidence of your worth.
- **Protects Your Mood**: You can face tough facts with less anger or despair, leaving room for calm problem-solving.

In fact, realistic thinking helps you handle issues more effectively. A mind locked in negativity might either blow up in anger or give up. A mind that sees possibilities can try new approaches without feeling trapped.

## Turning Negative Thoughts into Action Steps

Sometimes, your negative thoughts point to real concerns. For example, you might think, "My coworker does not respect me." While that might be an overstatement, there could be an underlying issue—maybe they interrupt you often. Once you challenge the negative label ("They are always disrespectful!"), you can create an action step: calmly talk to them about interruptions, or set a boundary. This transforms a looping negative thought into a plan for change, reducing anger because you are doing something constructive.

## Building a Support System

Changing how you think is easier if you have supportive people around. If you have a friend who also wants to think more positively, you can swap notes about your progress. You might check in daily, sharing a negative thought you caught and how you turned it around. Encouragement from others helps keep you motivated. If you feel stuck in a deep pattern of negative thinking, a counselor or therapist can guide you through methods to break free, giving you tools for your specific struggles.

---

## Handling Setbacks

It is normal to slip back into negative thinking now and then. When you notice you have spent an hour stewing in unhelpful thoughts, do not scold yourself. Instead:

1. **Recognize the Slip**: "I got caught in that all-or-nothing mindset again."
2. **Review**: "What triggered it this time? Was I hungry, tired, or stressed at work?"
3. **Refocus**: "Let me test these thoughts for fairness and find a more balanced view."
4. **Plan for Next Time**: "If this happens again, I will take a short walk or call a friend to reset."

Progress is not a straight line. Each slip offers a lesson about what triggers you, so you can prepare better.

---

## Keeping a Thought-Change Journal

A helpful exercise is to keep a small notebook or note app to track changes in your thinking. Each time you catch a negative thought, you can note:

- The situation
- The negative thought you noticed
- How you challenged it
- Your new, more balanced thought
- How you felt afterward

Reviewing this record shows you the progress you are making. Over time, you might spot patterns—like certain times of day or environments that spark the most negativity. You also see how your replacement thoughts help you feel calmer. Seeing these successes can inspire you to keep practicing.

## Real-Life Examples of Thought Shifts

Consider some short examples:

1. **Negative Thought**: "My friend is late again. She must not value my time."
   **Balanced Shift**: "She has been late before, but she might have a good reason today. Let me send a quick message to check if she's okay."
2. **Negative Thought**: "I messed up that presentation; my career is ruined."
   **Balanced Shift**: "I stumbled a bit, but maybe I can fix the errors. I have had some good presentations in the past, so not all is lost."
3. **Negative Thought**: "My kids never listen. I am a terrible parent."
   **Balanced Shift**: "They are not listening right now, but kids often test limits. Let me approach them calmly or try a different strategy."

In each case, the balanced thought does not pretend everything is perfect. It simply allows a calmer, more realistic approach that leaves less room for destructive anger.

## Tying Thought Changes to Anger Management Techniques

When you pair new thinking habits with the other anger management skills you have learned—like safe ways to express anger or conflict resolution steps—you build a stronger defense. For example, you might:

- **Pause and Breathe** when you notice a negative thought about someone at home. Then check that thought for fairness and try a more balanced view before responding.
- **Use Problem-Solving** if you see a negative thought is pointing to a real issue. Instead of letting anger boil, turn it into an action plan.
- **Practice Self-Care** if you notice that lack of sleep or hunger fuels negative thoughts. Getting enough rest or having healthy meals can reduce the power of those thoughts.

All these methods work together to lower the heat of anger and guide you toward healthier ways of thinking and behaving.

## Looking Ahead

Changing negative thoughts does not happen in a single day. It is a skill you refine over time. As you become more aware of your thinking patterns and practice replacing unhelpful ideas, you will likely see a drop in how often you feel intense anger. You might still get upset—it is natural—but your mindset will be more balanced, letting you handle conflict or stress without plunging into rage.

In the upcoming chapter, we will explore relaxation methods for anger control. These methods help soothe your body and mind, keeping negative thoughts from spiraling. When paired with the thought-shifting skills you are now learning, these relaxation strategies can further support a calmer, clearer approach to life's challenges. Even when things go wrong, you will have a mental toolbox to keep anger from dominating.

Stay patient with yourself as you practice these thinking changes. Each time you catch a negative thought and shift it, you are training your mind to react differently in the future. Over weeks and months, the shift can become more natural, allowing you to face stressful moments with far less anger clouding your decisions. You deserve a mind that is not weighed down by negativity—and working on your thinking patterns is a powerful step in creating that lighter inner space.

# Chapter 16: Relaxation Methods for Anger Control

When anger begins to build, your body can go into high alert: tense muscles, rapid heartbeat, tight chest, and shaky hands. This physical surge can make it harder to think clearly, pushing you closer to snapping. Practicing relaxation methods helps you counteract these tense feelings so you can calm down before anger explodes. In this chapter, we will look at simple techniques you can use at home, work, or anywhere else to settle your body and mind. By learning these methods, you give yourself tools to prevent anger from ruling your actions.

## Why Relaxation Methods Help with Anger

Anger triggers a "fight or flight" response in the body, releasing stress hormones like adrenaline. This is meant to help you face immediate threats. But in daily life, many anger triggers are not physical dangers. Even so, the stress response can flood your body. Relaxation methods work by:

1. **Slowing Your Breathing**
   When you breathe deeply and steadily, you send signals to your brain that it is okay to settle down.
2. **Loosening Muscles**
   Tension in the body fuels angry feelings. Relaxing your muscles can help cool that tension.
3. **Shifting Focus**
   Concentrating on a soothing exercise instead of the trigger can break the cycle of angry thoughts.
4. **Reducing Stress Hormones**
   Techniques like meditation or gentle movement can lower levels of stress chemicals in your body over time.

Think of relaxation as a tool to regain control. It does not erase the cause of your anger, but it gives you a clearer head to handle that cause in a healthier way.

## Deep Breathing Techniques

Deep breathing is one of the simplest and most effective ways to reduce tension quickly. Here are some methods to try:

1. **4-4-4 Breathing**
    - Inhale for a count of four.
    - Hold the breath for a count of four.
    - Exhale slowly for a count of four.
    - Repeat several times.
2. **5-7 Breathing**
    - Inhale for a count of five.
    - Exhale for a count of seven.
    - Keep going, letting your exhale be longer than your inhale. This helps calm the heart rate.
3. **Belly Breathing**
    - Place one hand on your chest and one on your belly.
    - Breathe in through your nose, feeling your belly expand under your hand.
    - Exhale through your mouth, feeling your belly fall.
    - Try to keep your chest still, focusing on deep belly movement.

As you breathe, pay attention to the cool air entering your nose and the warm air leaving your mouth. Focus on this sensation instead of angry thoughts. Just a minute or two of this can shift your mood.

---

## Progressive Muscle Relaxation (PMR)

This method involves tensing and then releasing muscle groups in your body. It helps you notice where you hold tension and let it go. Here is a basic way to do it:

1. **Find a Comfortable Position**
   Sit or lie down, loosen any tight clothing.
2. **Start with Your Feet**
   Curl your toes, squeeze them hard for about five seconds, then release. Feel the difference between tight and relaxed.

3. **Move Up the Body**
   Tighten your calves, then relax. Move to your thighs, your belly, your chest, your arms, and so on, all the way to your face. Spend a few seconds tensing each group before letting it go.
4. **Notice the Soothing Effect**
   After you finish, take a slow breath and see if your body feels looser. If some areas are still tense, repeat the process there.

Progressive Muscle Relaxation can be done quickly if you have only a little time. Even doing it for a couple of major muscle groups—like your shoulders and neck—can ease anger.

---

## Grounding Exercises

When anger takes hold, you may feel disconnected from the present moment. Grounding exercises bring your attention back to the here and now:

1. **5-4-3-2-1 Method**
   - Notice five things you can see around you (a table, a window, a plant, etc.).
   - Notice four things you can touch (your clothing, a pen, your hair, the chair).
   - Notice three things you can hear (traffic outside, a humming fan, quiet music).
   - Notice two things you can smell (perhaps your coffee or the scent of your lotion).
   - Notice one thing you can taste (if nothing is in your mouth, think about a taste you remember).
2. **Name the Colors**
   Look around and list colors you see. You could say, "Blue curtain, green couch, white lamp," until your mind feels calmer.
3. **Focus on an Object**
   Hold or look at a single object like a rock or a pencil. Notice its texture, weight, color. This simple focus can interrupt racing, angry thoughts.

Grounding can be done quietly in a public place without anyone noticing. It shifts your mind from "I am angry" to "I am present," which helps loosen anger's grip.

---

## Gentle Movement and Stretching

Physical tension can spark or worsen anger. Gentle movement helps release that tension:

1. **Neck Rolls**
   Slowly roll your head in a circle, stretching the neck muscles. Do this a few times clockwise, then switch direction.
2. **Shoulder Rolls**
   Raise your shoulders up to your ears, then roll them back and down. Repeat, rolling forward too. This eases shoulder tightness that often comes with anger.
3. **Arm Stretches**
   Extend your arms over your head, interlace your fingers, and gently stretch upward. Or place one hand behind your back, reaching between your shoulder blades, and use the other hand to apply slight pressure.
4. **Walking**
   If you can, take a short walk. Notice how your feet feel on the ground. Pay attention to your surroundings. Let each step release some of the tension.

These movements do not have to be lengthy or strenuous. A few mindful stretches can clear your mind, helping anger fade to a more manageable level.

---

## Visualization Techniques

Visualization taps into your imagination to calm you:

1. **Peaceful Scene**
   Close your eyes (if safe and appropriate to do so). Picture a place you find relaxing: a beach, a forest, a quiet room. Imagine the sights, sounds, and smells there. Breathe slowly, as if you are actually there.

2. **Safe Space**
   Invent a calm, safe space in your mind. It could be entirely imaginary—a glowing cave, a cozy cabin with a warm fire, or a floating bubble. Whenever anger builds, take a quick "visit" to this safe space in your imagination.
3. **Soft Colors**
   Picture yourself surrounded by a soothing color—blue, green, or whatever feels calming. Imagine the color gently swirling around you, easing your stress.

Visualization can shift your thoughts from the anger trigger to a calm mental image. With practice, this can be done quickly, even in the middle of a stressful situation.

---

## Music and Sound

Sounds can change your mood. The next time you feel anger rising, consider:

1. **Soft Music**
   If you have access to music, pick a track that calms you—instrumentals, nature sounds, or a gentle tune. Focus on the melody or beat instead of your angry thoughts.
2. **White Noise**
   Some people find steady sounds—like rain or a fan—soothing. You can find white noise apps or recordings online.
3. **Humming or Singing**
   Gently humming a tune or singing under your breath can relax the throat and chest area, which often tense up during anger. Even if it feels silly, it can interrupt the buildup of rage.

Be mindful of your surroundings—blasting music in a quiet office might not be appropriate. But headphones, if allowed, or stepping outside for a moment, can make this method work.

## Mindful Breathing Walk

If you can step outside or move to a less crowded area, try a mindful breathing walk:

1. **Walk Slowly**
   Do not rush. Let your arms hang loose or swing gently.
2. **Sync Steps with Breathing**
   For example, inhale for two steps, exhale for two steps. Adjust the count so it feels comfortable.
3. **Look Around**
   Notice what you see—trees, buildings, sky. Listen for birds or traffic. Feel the temperature of the air.
4. **Focus on Calm**
   If angry thoughts appear, note them briefly, then return your focus to your steps and breathing.

This combines movement, grounding, and mindfulness. A five-minute mindful walk can lower your body's stress response, making anger less intense.

---

## Quick Calming Checks for Busy Moments

Sometimes you need a fast method in the middle of daily tasks:

1. **Hand on Heart**
   Place one hand on your chest. Take three slow breaths, feeling your chest rise and fall. Remind yourself, "I am allowed to pause."
2. **Wrist Taps**
   Gently tap the inside of your wrist with two fingers from your other hand, feeling the small pulses. Concentrate on the tapping rhythm instead of your anger.
3. **Blink Slowly**
   Close your eyes for a moment, then open them slowly. Repeat this a few times. Visualize each blink as washing away a bit of anger.

These mini-exercises can be done in seconds, helping you regain control before you say something you might regret.

## Creating a Personal Relaxation Toolkit

It helps to have several go-to methods in your back pocket. After trying different techniques, pick the ones that fit your lifestyle. For example, you might decide:

- **At Home**: Use progressive muscle relaxation or gentle stretching.
- **At Work**: Practice 4-4-4 breathing or wrist taps if you cannot leave your desk.
- **With Kids or Family**: Go for a short mindful walk or do simple grounding exercises together.

Having a "toolkit" of methods ensures you are prepared. You can even write them on a small card or keep a list on your phone to remind yourself.

---

## Regular Practice for Better Results

Relaxation skills work best when you practice them regularly, not just during anger spikes. If you build them into your daily routine, you become better at calming yourself quickly. Some ways to practice:

- **Morning Routine**: Spend a couple of minutes doing deep breathing before you start your day.
- **Break Times**: Use a short break at work or school to do a quick visualization or stretch.
- **Before Bed**: Do progressive muscle relaxation to help you sleep.

This consistent use lowers your overall stress levels, making it less likely that anger will catch you off guard.

---

## Combining Relaxation with Other Anger Skills

Relaxation does not fix every problem that causes anger, but it creates a better mental state to address those problems. For example, if you have a conflict with a coworker, you might:

1. **Relax First**: Use a breathing exercise to calm your body so you do not enter the conversation ready to explode.
2. **Use Assertive Communication**: Explain your concerns calmly, using "I" statements.
3. **Stay Grounded**: If anger flares again mid-talk, you can use a quick wrist tap or mindful breathing to keep from yelling.

By pairing calmness with respectful conversation, you improve the odds of resolving issues without harming relationships.

---

## Cautions and Limitations

- **Seek Medical Advice if Needed**: Some relaxation methods might not be suitable for people with certain health conditions, such as severe anxiety or breathing problems. If you have any doubts, talk to a health professional.
- **Be Patient**: If you have intense anger or deep-rooted triggers, these methods may only help part of the way. Additional support from therapy or counseling might be needed.
- **Avoid Using Relaxation to Ignore Problems**: Relaxing is meant to help you handle stress, not to hide from real issues. Use the calm state you gain to address underlying causes of anger.

---

## Teaching Others

If you find certain methods helpful, you might share them with friends or family. You can:

- **Practice Together**: Doing a group relaxation, like a short guided breathing session, can reduce overall tension in a household.
- **Show Kids Basic Exercises**: Children who learn to breathe deeply or ground themselves can manage anger better, preventing tantrums and fights.
- **Suggest Workplace Breaks**: If you have supportive coworkers, propose a two-minute breathing exercise during stressful times.

Teaching others can also reinforce your own habit of using these methods.

---

## What to Do If Relaxation Methods Fail in the Moment

Sometimes, anger can escalate so quickly that you cannot calm down immediately. If that happens:

1. **Remove Yourself**
   If possible, step away from the situation to prevent an outburst. This could mean going to another room or, if at work, walking to the restroom.
2. **Give It Time**
   Some anger passes with a little time. Once you cool off a bit, try a technique again.
3. **Seek Support**
   If you are with someone you trust, let them know you are feeling overwhelmed and angry. They might give you space or help you talk through it calmly.

Remember, it is okay not to get it right every time. Each instance teaches you more about what works and what might need adjusting.

---

## Long-Term Benefits of Relaxation for Anger

When you practice these methods often, you will likely notice:

- **Lower Overall Stress**: You might handle day-to-day hassles with more ease.
- **Better Emotional Control**: Fewer explosive moments and more measured responses.
- **Improved Health**: Chronic anger and stress can harm your body, so keeping calm can support better sleep, mood, and physical well-being.
- **Kinder Relationships**: Loved ones may appreciate that you are less reactive, leading to warmer, more trusting connections.

None of these changes happen overnight, but each time you choose to relax instead of yell, you move closer to a more peaceful life.

## Pairing Relaxation with Healthy Habits

Relaxation works best when your overall lifestyle supports it. Consider adding:

- **Regular Exercise**: Activities like walking, yoga, or cycling release tension and lift your mood.
- **Adequate Sleep**: Being well-rested lowers irritability.
- **Balanced Diet**: Feeling shaky from hunger or eating too much junk can worsen mood swings.
- **Limiting Caffeine and Alcohol**: Both can affect your nervous system and make anger spikes more frequent.

A balanced body often has an easier time staying calm under stress.

## Making Relaxation a Lifelong Skill

Think of relaxation methods as skills you keep refining. As life changes, you might find new challenges or triggers that spark anger. By maintaining a habit of relaxation, you stay flexible and ready to adapt. Over time, you might discover you handle conflicts far better than you did before. You could also experiment with more advanced methods like guided imagery, gentle forms of martial arts, or mindful breathing apps. The key is to remain open to learning and practicing, knowing that mastery grows with each attempt.

# Chapter 17: Avoiding Common Anger Triggers

Sometimes, it feels like anger appears without warning. You might be in a calm mood, then something happens that sets off an angry reaction. However, anger rarely comes from nowhere. It is often linked to triggers—people, places, events, or actions that nudge you toward frustration. In this chapter, we will examine how to identify and avoid these common anger triggers. By reducing your exposure to triggers or handling them more effectively, you can help keep anger in check. Although you cannot eliminate every trigger in life, you can develop tactics to face them with less stress.

---

## What Are Anger Triggers?

An anger trigger is anything that pushes your emotions toward anger. It can be a specific situation, like a crowded bus or a demanding boss. It can be something someone says or does, or even a thought that pops into your mind. Triggers vary from person to person. One individual might have no issue with loud noises, while another finds them extremely upsetting.

These triggers become problems when they are frequent or intense enough to make you explode with anger. Recognizing them is the first step. You cannot manage what you cannot see. Sometimes, a trigger is obvious (like an insult), and other times, it is subtle (like a certain tone of voice reminding you of an unpleasant memory).

---

## Why Identifying Triggers Matters

1. **Prevention**
   If you know what sets you off, you can steer clear of it when possible. For instance, if you often lose your temper in the grocery store at peak hours, you can shop at a quieter time. Simple changes like this can reduce angry incidents.
2. **Planning**
   Even if you cannot avoid a trigger, knowing it is coming helps you

prepare. You might practice deep breathing or brief stretches before heading into a stressful event.
3. **Awareness of Patterns**
Tracking triggers can reveal bigger life patterns—like which relationships, tasks, or situations create consistent anger. This knowledge can guide you to make changes in how you live or how you handle conflicts.
4. **Control Over Reactions**
When a trigger hits you out of nowhere, you might lash out without thinking. Once you recognize the trigger, you can slow down. You can pause and decide on a calmer response instead of an instant eruption.

Identifying triggers puts you in the driver's seat. Anger feels less random when you see the cause behind it.

---

## Common Types of Anger Triggers

Triggers can be split into a few broad categories:

1. **Environmental Triggers**
    - **Noise and Crowds**: Some people get tense in loud, packed settings.
    - **Traffic and Delays**: Feeling stuck on the road or facing cancellations can spark anger.
    - **Extreme Temperatures**: Being too hot or cold can test anyone's patience.
2. **Interpersonal Triggers**
    - **Criticism or Teasing**: Harsh words, even if meant as a joke, can stir up anger.
    - **Disrespect**: Feeling ignored or belittled may lead you to snap.
    - **Different Communication Styles**: For example, if you hate yelling and someone raises their voice at you, that might be a major trigger.
3. **Internal Triggers**
    - **Pain or Discomfort**: Chronic pain, tiredness, or hunger can lower your ability to cope.
    - **Negative Self-Talk**: Thoughts like "I cannot do anything right" can fuel anger at both yourself and the world.

- **Memories**: A past event might replay in your mind, triggering anger if something in the present resembles that memory.
4. **Situational Triggers**
    - **Unmet Expectations**: For instance, you expect a coworker to finish a task by noon, but they fail to do so. This mismatch can cause anger.
    - **Tight Deadlines**: Feeling rushed or overloaded with responsibilities can bring irritability.
    - **Financial Stress**: Worry about money can make you more prone to snapping over small things.

Being aware of these groups can help you reflect on which ones affect you the most.

---

## Identifying Your Personal Triggers

1. **Keep an Anger Log**
   When you feel anger building, write down the circumstances: where you were, who was there, what was happening, what you were thinking. Over time, patterns will emerge. You might notice you often get angry after skipping lunch, or when you talk to a certain family member.
2. **Ask Trusted People**
   Sometimes, friends or family see our triggers more clearly than we do. You can ask, "Have you noticed what usually sets me off?" They might mention repeated scenarios you were unaware of.
3. **Reflect on Recent Outbursts**
   Think about your last few angry moments. What sparked each one? Look for similarities, such as being interrupted or feeling left out.
4. **Notice Physical Reactions**
   If your heart races when someone brings up a specific topic, that is a sign it might be a trigger. Bodily cues can warn you before your mind fully registers what is bothering you.

As you gather this information, you begin to see which situations or behaviors reliably push you toward anger.

---

## Strategies for Avoiding or Reducing Triggers

1. **Alter Your Routine**
   If you hate crowded stores, shop at off-peak hours. If rush-hour traffic makes you rage, see if you can shift your commute times or work from home part of the day. Changing routines can spare you from frequent frustrations.
2. **Set Boundaries**
   If certain people trigger you by bringing up sensitive topics, set boundaries: "I do not wish to discuss that subject." If it is a coworker who constantly criticizes you, talk to them or a supervisor about how you can keep the conversation more respectful.
3. **Plan for Stressful Situations**
   Sometimes you cannot avoid a trigger, like a family gathering with relatives who argue. Prepare in advance: practice relaxation methods, bring someone supportive with you, or decide on a polite excuse to leave early if conflict arises.
4. **Manage Physical Needs**
   Address basic needs that can amplify anger, like hunger and tiredness. Carry a snack if missing a meal sets you off. Schedule breaks if you get short-tempered when overworked.
5. **Limit Exposure to Negative Stimuli**
   Constantly watching upsetting news or reading harsh online comments might keep you in a tense state. Cut down on these sources of stress if possible, or only consume them at specific, planned times.

Small adjustments can drastically reduce how often you face your biggest anger triggers.

---

## Handling Persistent Triggers

Some triggers cannot be avoided—like a chronic health issue, essential tasks at work, or a family member who lives with you. In these cases, focus on coping instead:

1. **Develop a Coping Plan**
   Write down steps you will take when the trigger appears. For example:

- Recognize you are entering a triggering situation.
- Use deep breathing or a quick walk.
- Keep your self-talk balanced, reminding yourself you can handle this.
- If anger escalates, take a brief time-out.

2. **Practice Acceptance**
   If the trigger cannot change, accepting it might be key. Acceptance does not mean you approve of it, but rather that you acknowledge reality and focus on what you can control—your response.
3. **Seek Support**
   If your trigger is an ongoing problem—such as a health issue or a tense living situation—talk to a counselor, support group, or trusted friend. Sharing the burden can reduce the sense of frustration.
4. **Reframe the Trigger**
   Sometimes, shifting how you view a trigger helps. If a coworker's behavior annoys you, you might tell yourself, "They are going through something tough," or "I can use this as practice for staying calm." This does not excuse bad behavior, but it stops you from seeing it as purely malicious.

Persisting triggers require more patience and creativity, but with the right tools, you can lessen their impact on your mood.

---

## Handling Anger Triggered by People

When your triggers center on certain individuals, it can feel complicated because relationships have emotional layers. However, you can still apply strategies:

1. **Calm Communication**
   If someone's words or actions consistently make you angry, consider talking to them when you are calm. Use "I" statements to share how you feel. For instance, "I feel upset when I am interrupted during a meeting. Can we agree to let each other finish speaking?"
2. **Set Up Boundaries**
   Limit how much time you spend with a toxic friend or relative. If the person lives in your home, designate personal space or quiet hours where you do not engage.

3. **Use a Mediator**
   If direct talks fail, a mediator (like a neutral friend, family counselor, or workplace mediator) might help. Sometimes having a third party present fosters more respectful dialogue.
4. **Develop Empathy**
   At times, understanding why someone acts a certain way can reduce anger. They may be dealing with stress, fear, or a personal problem you do not know about. This does not mean you accept harmful behavior, but empathy can soften the edge of your frustration.

People-based triggers often require careful handling of emotions. Balancing firmness with respect can lower tension on both sides.

---

## Dealing with Unexpected Triggers

You might plan your day to avoid stress, yet anger flares when something unexpected happens: a sudden car breakdown, a rude comment from a stranger, or an unexpected bill. For these surprise triggers:

1. **Pause, If Possible**
   Give yourself a few seconds to breathe before reacting. This short gap can prevent you from snapping.
2. **Assess the Real Impact**
   Ask yourself: "Is this really huge, or does it just feel huge?" Sometimes, the shock intensifies anger. Breaking down the problem into small steps can ease that sense of panic or rage.
3. **Seek Quick Solutions**
   If your car breaks down, call for roadside assistance immediately. Taking swift action can make you feel less helpless, cooling your anger. If someone says something rude, you can choose to walk away instead of engaging.
4. **Stay Flexible**
   Life is full of surprises. Adopting a flexible mindset—recognizing that plans can change—builds resilience. When you accept that not everything goes smoothly, you reduce the friction that fuels anger.

Unexpected triggers test your ability to adapt. Over time, practicing calm responses will make these sudden shocks less likely to set you off.

---

## Internal States That Amplify Triggers

Certain internal states make you more prone to anger, regardless of the external trigger:

1. **Stress Overload**
   If you are already juggling many responsibilities, even a small extra task might push you to anger.
2. **Poor Sleep**
   Lack of rest undermines emotional control. When you are tired, you have less patience and are quicker to see threats or annoyances.
3. **Low Blood Sugar**
   When you have not eaten, your body craves energy. This can make you edgy and less able to cope with stress.
4. **Anxiety or Depression**
   Ongoing mental health struggles can lower your threshold for frustration. If you are already feeling anxious or sad, triggers might hit harder.

Tending to your overall well-being—through rest, proper nutrition, and mental health support—raises your anger threshold. You become less vulnerable to triggers because your emotional reserves are not already drained.

---

## Gradual Exposure for Certain Triggers

If a trigger severely disrupts your life but cannot be fully avoided, sometimes gradual exposure can help you build tolerance:

1. **Define Small Steps**
   For example, if large crowds terrify you, start by going to a moderately busy store for a short visit. Then build up to busier places as you feel ready.

2. **Practice Coping Tools**
   Before each exposure, rehearse your relaxation and self-talk methods. This way, you have a plan to keep anger or panic under control.
3. **Reward Progress**
   Give yourself a small treat or positive acknowledgment after facing a trigger in a calmer way than before. Recognize your effort in staying composed.
4. **Reflect on Growth**
   After each exposure, note what helped you remain less angry or stressed. Over time, this practice can make even intense triggers more manageable.

This technique is often used in addressing anxieties, but it can also apply to anger triggers, especially if they involve particular fears or environments.

---

## Shifting Your Outlook on Triggers

Instead of viewing triggers as enemies you must avoid at all costs, try seeing them as clues about your needs or boundaries. For instance:

- If you get angry when coworkers ignore your suggestions, it might signal you value respect and recognition.
- If you snap when your partner leaves things messy, it might mean you need organization for peace of mind.

By reframing triggers as signposts, you can take steps to fulfill these needs (e.g., seeking a workplace where opinions are heard or setting a routine with your partner for household tasks). This approach moves you from feeling victimized by triggers to actively addressing underlying needs.

---

## Communication About Triggers

If family or friends often unwittingly trigger your anger, open communication can help:

1. **Explain Briefly**
   "When I hear loud chewing, I feel on edge. I know it sounds small, but it sets me off."
2. **Ask for Small Adjustments**
   "Could you avoid chewing gum in the shared office space, please?"
3. **Offer Appreciation**
   If they respect your request, thank them. This builds goodwill and encourages more cooperation in the future.
4. **Acknowledge Their Comfort Too**
   "I know it might be inconvenient, but it means a lot that you are trying."

This approach fosters mutual respect, rather than leaving them guessing why you seem irritated.

---

## Choosing Which Triggers to Tolerate

Not every trigger can or should be removed. Sometimes, facing minor annoyances can build resilience. If you always avoid any hint of discomfort, you might shrink your world too much. Decide which triggers are worth managing and which you can let slide. For example:

- **Worth Managing**: Chronic disrespect, unsafe conditions, or situations that truly harm your well-being.
- **Worth Tolerating**: The occasional slow line at the coffee shop, mild disagreements, or typical daily noises.

Striking a balance between healthy boundaries and reasonable tolerance keeps life from becoming too restricted while still respecting your emotional needs.

---

## The Role of Self-Care in Trigger Management

When you practice good self-care, triggers lose some of their power. Self-care includes:

- **Adequate Sleep**: Aim for consistent rest so you start each day with better emotional balance.

- **Balanced Nutrition**: Steady blood sugar helps you keep calm. Avoid skipping meals.
- **Physical Activity**: Exercise releases tension and can lighten your mood, making triggers less overwhelming.
- **Relaxation Breaks**: Short, daily relaxation exercises keep your stress level lower overall.
- **Mindful Moments**: Periodically pause to check your feelings and thoughts, preventing built-up frustration.

Self-care provides a strong foundation for dealing with triggers without snapping.

## Handling Multiple Triggers at Once

Sometimes triggers pile up—maybe you are stuck in traffic (environmental trigger), feeling hungry (internal trigger), and you have a phone call from a critical boss (interpersonal trigger). In these moments:

1. **Address the Immediate Physical Need**
   If possible, grab a quick snack or pull over to breathe for a minute.
2. **Reduce One Trigger**
   Turn off an annoying radio station, or politely ask your boss if you can call back in a few minutes.
3. **Use Calming Techniques**
   Do a brief grounding or breathing exercise to lower overall stress.
4. **Handle One Issue at a Time**
   Do not try to solve everything at once. Focus on the biggest trigger first, then move on to the next.

When triggers stack, it can feel overwhelming, but breaking them down can prevent a total meltdown.

## When Professional Help Is Needed

If triggers dominate your daily life and small adjustments are not enough, you may benefit from talking to a counselor or therapist. This is especially true if:

- You feel angry almost all the time.
- Triggers cause severe fights or harm relationships.
- Avoidance is shrinking your world.
- You have symptoms of other mental health issues, like severe anxiety or depression.

A professional can help you explore deep-seated causes, develop coping strategies, and improve emotional regulation. Therapy is not a sign of weakness; it is a resource for better living.

## Practicing Gratitude Around Potential Triggers

It may sound odd, but pairing gratitude with tricky situations can change your mindset. For example:

- If traffic is your trigger, think: "At least I have a car and a job to go to."
- If a family member's words annoy you, recall a moment they were supportive.

This does not mean ignoring the frustration. Instead, it balances your view, reminding you that life has positives. A balanced view can keep anger from spiraling out of control.

## Checking Your Progress

As you work on avoiding or handling triggers, track your progress:

1. **Reflect Weekly**
   Note if certain triggers bother you less than before. Celebrate small improvements like keeping calm in a situation that once set you off.
2. **Adjust Strategies**
   If one approach is not working, try another. Maybe you need a longer pre-event relaxation routine or a clearer boundary-setting conversation.
3. **Acknowledge Mistakes**
   If you fail to avoid or manage a trigger and blow up, do not despair. Learn

from it. Figure out what went wrong and how you can prepare differently next time.

Progress is usually gradual. Each small step indicates you are moving toward healthier anger management.

---

## Staying Flexible

Life changes, and triggers can evolve. A new job might introduce different stressors, or an old trigger might fade. Remain open to ongoing adjustments. Keep paying attention to your reactions, and do not assume you have everything figured out permanently. Flexibility helps you adapt to new environments and personal growth.

---

# Chapter 18: Releasing Anger Through Forgiveness

Anger can linger in the mind and body long after a conflict or betrayal occurs. Sometimes, the best way to free yourself from that lingering anger is through forgiveness. But forgiveness can be misunderstood. It does not mean you approve of what happened or let someone continue harmful behavior. Instead, forgiveness is about choosing to let go of the anger, resentment, or bitterness that weighs you down. In this chapter, we will explore what forgiveness really is, why it can help reduce anger, and how to approach it—whether you are forgiving someone else or yourself.

## What Is Forgiveness?

Forgiveness is the internal act of releasing negative feelings about someone who hurt you (or about yourself if you made a mistake). It is a choice not to hold onto anger or seek revenge. People sometimes fear that forgiving means saying the hurtful action was acceptable, but that is not the case. Forgiveness is separate from excusing or forgetting. You can forgive while still recognizing the harm done. You can also forgive someone while deciding not to have a close relationship with them if they remain unsafe or harmful.

## Why Forgiveness Matters for Anger

1. **Breaking the Anger Cycle**
   When you refuse to forgive, you might replay the event in your mind. Each replay can reignite your anger, locking you in a cycle of resentment.
2. **Emotional Healing**
   Holding onto anger creates emotional stress that can affect your sleep, mood, and relationships. Forgiveness can relieve that burden, bringing more emotional peace.
3. **Physical Benefits**
   Chronic anger can lead to tense muscles, high blood pressure, and other

health problems. Forgiveness, by easing anger, can support better physical health.
4. **Improved Relationships**
Forgiveness can pave the way for repaired bonds, though it does not guarantee full trust immediately. If both sides are willing to change and respect each other, forgiveness can help heal rifts.

By choosing forgiveness, you give yourself the gift of reduced anger and stress, regardless of whether the other person seeks forgiveness.

---

## Understanding the Difference Between Forgiveness and Reunion

Some people assume that if they forgive, they must welcome the person back into their life as before. However, you can forgive while keeping boundaries:

- **Forgiveness**: You let go of resentment and the desire to retaliate. You choose not to allow anger to control your thoughts about this person.
- **Reunion or Reconciliation**: This involves trust and cooperation from both parties. It requires that the person who hurt you shows genuine change or remorse if they want a renewed relationship.

You can release your anger while still maintaining distance if that person continues to behave harmfully. This distinction lets you see forgiveness as a personal choice for your well-being, not an obligation to ignore wrongdoing.

---

## Deciding to Forgive

Forgiveness is a process and does not happen instantly:

1. **Acknowledge the Harm**
   You do not have to deny that you were hurt. Recognize what happened and how it made you feel.
2. **Own Your Feelings**
   Let yourself feel the anger, sadness, or betrayal. Pushing these feelings away can lead to buried anger. Instead, allow them to surface in a safe way—by journaling, talking to a friend, or working with a therapist.

3. **Assess the Situation**
   Ask yourself: "Is holding onto this anger helping me or hurting me?" If it only causes pain and cannot fix anything, you might decide forgiveness is healthier than clinging to resentment.
4. **Commit to Letting Go**
   Forgiveness is a choice. You might say to yourself, "I am ready to free myself from this anger." This commitment might need to be renewed repeatedly if old anger resurfaces.

Deciding to forgive does not minimize the hurt. It is about shifting from feeling hostage to anger to choosing emotional freedom.

---

## Steps Toward Forgiving Others

1. **Reflect on the Other Person's Humanity**
   The one who hurt you is not just the sum of that hurtful action. They have flaws and may be acting from ignorance, fear, or their own pain. Recognizing their human complexity can soften some of the anger.
2. **Consider Possible Explanations**
   This does not mean justifying wrongdoing. But understanding why they acted as they did might reduce the intensity of your anger. For example, maybe they lied out of fear of losing your respect.
3. **Release the Need for Payback**
   Forgiveness involves letting go of revenge fantasies or hoping they will suffer. You decide you will not keep stoking that anger.
4. **Find Meaning in the Experience**
   Sometimes, you can learn about your boundaries, self-worth, or empathy through a painful event. This does not excuse the harm, but it can allow you to gain personal insight.
5. **Perform a Forgiveness Ritual (If Helpful)**
   Some people write a letter (not necessarily sent) describing the hurt and stating they choose to forgive. Others might release their anger symbolically, like throwing a stone into a river while imagining the resentment leaving them.

If anger returns later, remind yourself of your decision to forgive and repeat steps as needed.

## Forgiving Yourself

Self-directed anger can be as strong as anger toward others. Perhaps you regret a past choice, a hurtful action, or a failure to protect yourself. Self-forgiveness follows a similar path:

1. **Admit the Mistake**
   Pretending it never happened blocks self-forgiveness. Acknowledge what you did and why you feel guilty or ashamed.
2. **Learn from the Error**
   Ask: "What can I do better next time?" or "How can I repair any damage?" If you owe someone an apology, consider offering it sincerely.
3. **Accept Your Imperfection**
   Being human involves mistakes. Self-forgiveness involves compassion for the flawed, learning part of yourself.
4. **Release the Shame**
   Shame says, "I am a bad person." But you can do bad actions without being bad at your core. Once you fix what you can, carrying shame does not help you grow. Set it down.
5. **Affirm Self-Worth**
   Remind yourself that you deserve understanding and kindness, just like anyone else who messes up. Negative thoughts like "I am worthless" only keep anger directed at yourself.

Self-forgiveness can be challenging if you have high standards or have been taught you must be perfect. But letting go of self-anger frees you to move forward more positively.

---

## The Emotional Journey of Forgiveness

Forgiveness often moves through stages:

1. **Hurt and Shock**
   You discover the betrayal or harm. Anger, sadness, or disbelief might dominate.
2. **Denial or Detachment**
   You might try to ignore it or detach emotionally, unsure how to respond.

3. **Deep Anger or Resentment**
   You feel the weight of what happened. You might replay it in your head, fueling anger.
4. **Exploration of Understanding**
   Gradually, you start questioning if you want to hold onto this anger. You explore why the situation occurred or how to break free from these negative feelings.
5. **Decision to Forgive**
   You choose to release the resentment, even if it does not vanish instantly. You might have to reaffirm this choice multiple times.
6. **Ongoing Practice**
   Forgiveness is rarely one and done. Anger might creep back; you remind yourself of your choice. Over time, the anger often subsides for longer periods until it no longer dominates your emotional life.

Understanding these stages can help you be patient with yourself. It is normal to linger in some stages longer than others.

---

## Obstacles to Forgiveness

1. **Fear of Being Hurt Again**
   You might think forgiving means letting your guard down, so you stay angry as a form of self-protection. However, you can forgive and still keep boundaries.
2. **Belief That Anger Motivates You**
   Some people feel that staying angry gives them energy or drive. But this constant anger can damage health and relationships. Healthy motivation can come from resolve and clarity, not chronic rage.
3. **Doubting the Other Person's Sincerity**
   If you think they will never change, you might resist forgiving them. But recall that forgiveness is primarily for your sake, not theirs.
4. **Pride or Ego**
   Sometimes, pride can stop you from letting go. You might feel that forgiving is "giving in." But actually, forgiveness can be an act of strength, asserting your choice not to be ruled by anger.
5. **Confusion with Reconciliation**
   You might resist forgiveness because you do not want to resume contact.

Remember, you can forgive internally while still choosing limited or no contact.

Recognizing these obstacles can help you address them directly, making forgiveness more attainable.

---

## The Role of Apologies in Forgiveness

When someone apologizes sincerely, it can make forgiveness easier. A good apology involves admitting the wrongdoing, expressing regret, and committing to change. However, many people do not receive a proper apology from those who hurt them. In such cases:

- You can still choose to forgive for your own peace, even if they do not repent.
- An apology is not required for you to move forward.
- If they do offer an apology that seems incomplete, you can decide how much weight to give it. Some might apologize only to avoid guilt, but that does not invalidate your own process of letting go.

Forgiveness does not depend on anyone else's actions. It is your personal path to releasing anger.

---

## Forgiveness in Ongoing Relationships

When you need to keep interacting with someone who hurt you—like a family member, coworker, or friend—applying forgiveness might require ongoing effort:

1. **Communicate Boundaries**
   Let them know what behaviors are not acceptable. You can forgive but still insist that certain patterns must change.
2. **Ask for Changes**
   If they want to repair the relationship, suggest ways they can demonstrate respect or trustworthiness.
3. **Watch for Progress**
   Forgiveness does not mean ignoring harmful patterns. Keep an eye on whether they uphold their part of improving the relationship.

4. **Practice Self-Care**
   If tension remains, take steps to manage stress: talk to supportive friends, use relaxation methods, or seek counseling.

Forgiveness in a long-term relationship is often a mutual effort. But if only you commit to healthier behavior, you might still find personal peace, even if the relationship remains limited.

---

## Expressing Forgiveness (or Keeping It Private)

You do not always have to tell the person you forgive them, especially if contact is unsafe. Forgiveness can happen silently within you. However, in some contexts, sharing your choice can be healing:

- **Written or Spoken Statement**: "I have been holding anger about your actions. I want you to know I am choosing to let that anger go, though I still need to see changes from you to trust again."
- **Indirect Communication**: If direct contact is not wise, you might write a letter you do not send, or you might release resentment through a symbolic act.

Whether public or private, the essence is the same: letting go of sustained anger for your own emotional health.

---

## Forgiving the Deceased or Unreachable

Sometimes, the person who harmed you may be deceased or impossible to reach. You can still forgive in these situations:

1. **Write a Letter Never Sent**
   Pour out your feelings, acknowledge the hurt, and state your choice to let go of anger. Then keep or destroy the letter as you see fit.
2. **Engage in a Symbolic Ritual**
   You might speak aloud what you wish you could tell them, or place a note near a grave or memorial. This can provide closure even if they are not present.

3. **Seek Support if Needed**
   A counselor can guide you through unresolved anger toward someone who is no longer around. Group therapy or friends can also lend a listening ear.

Forgiveness here can be especially freeing, since there is no way for the person to apologize or explain.

---

## Combining Forgiveness with Other Anger Management Skills

Forgiveness does not replace the strategies you learned in previous chapters—like avoiding triggers, using relaxation techniques, or practicing healthier communication. Instead, it complements them:

- **When Triggers Occur**: You might realize your anger partly stems from an old wound you have not forgiven. Work on that forgiveness to weaken the trigger's grip.
- **Safe Anger Expression**: You can still express anger constructively about a current situation even as you work on forgiving past hurts.
- **Ongoing Self-Awareness**: Keep an eye on whether your feelings of resentment creep back. If they do, revisit your forgiveness decision.

All these tools support each other to form a more complete approach to anger management.

---

## What If Forgiveness Feels Impossible?

Some hurts run extremely deep—trauma, abuse, major betrayals. In such cases, the idea of forgiveness might feel unbearable. Remember:

1. **Take Your Time**
   There is no deadline for forgiveness. Rushing yourself might lead to fake forgiveness that does not truly heal you.
2. **Seek Professional Help**
   Therapy can help you process trauma and explore whether forgiveness is

the right path. A counselor can guide you carefully through the emotional layers.
3. **Focus on Safety First**
If you are still in a harmful situation, get out or protect yourself before worrying about forgiveness.
4. **Consider Partial Forgiveness**
Sometimes, you can let go of some anger but not all. Even partial release of bitterness can lighten your mental load.

Forgiveness is personal. In severe cases, it may be less about full forgiveness and more about finding a way to reduce anger's grip so you can live in peace.

---

## Signs You Are Moving Toward Forgiveness

1. **Reduced Resentment**
You notice you are not dwelling on revenge or replaying the hurt as often.
2. **More Emotional Calm**
Thinking of the person or event does not raise your blood pressure like before.
3. **Willingness to Consider Their View**
You might feel you can see nuances, even if you still do not agree with their actions.
4. **Feeling Lighter**
You sense a burden lifted. The anger you carried feels less heavy day by day.

These signs can be small at first, but they show that your mind is letting go of deep-seated anger.

---

## Maintaining Forgiveness Over Time

Anger can flare up again if something reminds you of the hurt. To maintain forgiveness:

- **Remind Yourself of the Decision**: "I have chosen to let go of this anger for my own good."

- **Use Relaxation Tools**: If thoughts of old hurts return, calm your body and mind.
- **Re-evaluate Boundaries**: If the person continues harmful actions, reinforce or adjust boundaries to prevent further damage.
- **Talk It Out**: A supportive friend or counselor can help you reaffirm your forgiveness if doubts arise.

Forgiveness is not a single moment; it is a continuing stance of releasing anger for the sake of your well-being.

# Chapter 19: Staying Calm in Public Settings

For many women, anger can rise quickly in public spaces. You might be waiting in a long line at the store, dealing with slow service at a busy restaurant, or riding a crowded bus when something sets you off. In public, it can feel more awkward to show anger, because strangers are watching. But it can also feel more stressful, because you have less control over your environment. This chapter will focus on ways to remain calm when you are out in public. We will look at how to handle tense moments, keep your composure, and walk away with minimal upset.

---

## The Challenges of Public Anger

Anger in public can carry extra pressure:

1. **Limited Privacy**
   You might worry about making a scene in front of strangers. This can make you hold in your anger until it explodes, or feel embarrassed if you do raise your voice.
2. **Crowded Spaces**
   Busy areas—like trains or busy streets—can lead to sensory overload. Loud noises, pushing crowds, and standing for long periods can make you feel on edge.
3. **Random Triggers**
   You do not know who you will encounter in public, so surprises can happen: a rude comment, someone cutting in line, or an unexpected delay.
4. **Fear of Judgment**
   You might think, "I do not want people to see me lose my temper." The fear of being labeled as "out of control" can worsen stress if you already feel anger boiling.

For these reasons, it is worth planning how to manage anger before stepping into places that often raise your blood pressure.

---

## Recognizing Your Public Anger Warning Signs

Your body and mind often give signals before you reach your limit in public:

- **Physical Tension**: Your shoulders may stiffen, your jaw might clench, and your breathing could get shallow.
- **Irritable Thoughts**: You notice yourself thinking, "Why is this line so slow?" "These people are so annoying," or "I need to get out of here."
- **Rising Restlessness**: You might tap your foot repeatedly or pace around.
- **Facial Expressions**: Scowling or glaring without realizing it.

If you spot these signs, it means you are heading toward an angry state. It is easier to act early than to wait until you snap.

---

## Preparing for Potentially Stressful Outings

Before going into a setting that often triggers anger—such as a busy shopping center or a lengthy doctor's appointment—try these steps:

1. **Set Realistic Expectations**
   Tell yourself, "It might be crowded or slow today. I will be patient and use my coping tools." If you expect a perfect, smooth outing, frustration can spike quickly when reality differs.
2. **Check Basic Needs**
   Hunger, thirst, or fatigue can lower your patience. Have a snack, bring water, or get a decent rest before you head out.
3. **Carry Quick Calming Aids**
   Some people keep a small stress ball, a calming scent, or headphones to play soothing music if things get tense. Having these items on hand can provide relief without drawing attention.
4. **Plan Your Time**
   If you rush or if you are on a tight schedule, you are more likely to feel anger when things slow you down. Build in extra minutes to wait in lines or deal with traffic, so a small delay does not ruin your day.
5. **Wear Comfortable Clothes**
   Shoes that hurt or clothing that is too tight can increase physical

discomfort and lead to irritability. Comfort reduces background stress in public spaces.

By preparing, you set a foundation for handling stressors without blowing up at strangers or feeling overwhelmed.

---

## Strategies for Calming Down on the Spot

When you feel anger rising in public, you can use several subtle methods to regain composure:

1. **Deep Breathing**
   Take a quiet breath in through your nose for a few counts, then exhale slowly through your mouth. You can do this in line or while waiting for a bus without anyone noticing.
2. **Grounding Exercise**
   Silently list five things you can see, four things you can feel, three things you can hear, two things you can smell, and one thing you can taste (if you have a mint or gum). This shifts focus away from anger.
3. **Repeat a Calming Phrase**
   In your mind, say something like, "I can stay calm," or "I will get through this." A short phrase can anchor you in a calmer mindset.
4. **Muscle Relaxation**
   If you can, tense and release a muscle group—like squeezing your fists, then letting go. This helps channel that angry energy without making a scene.
5. **Take a Step Back**
   If someone is too close or if the crowd is overwhelming, see if you can move a few steps away to get a bit of personal space. Even a small shift can reduce tension.

These quick techniques reduce the chance of lashing out. They also keep your mind busy with something positive instead of letting anger build.

---

## Dealing with Rude or Difficult Strangers

Encounters with rude strangers can spike your anger. Here is how to handle them in a calmer way:

1. **Pause Before Responding**
   A brief pause stops you from saying something harsh you might regret. If the person's words or tone upset you, count to three silently. Give yourself that tiny space to think.
2. **Decide on a Response**
   - **Ignore**: If it is a minor slight, ignoring might be the best option. Often, rude strangers just want a reaction.
   - **Speak Briefly**: If you must respond, keep it calm and short: "Please do not speak to me that way," or "That comment is not okay."
   - **Walk Away**: If the situation is escalating, leaving might be the safest. No argument is worth risking your well-being.
3. **Avoid Personal Attacks**
   If you choose to speak, focus on the behavior, not the person's character. Insulting them can fuel more anger on both sides.
4. **Seek Help If Threatened**
   If someone's behavior goes beyond rude and you feel unsafe, seek a staff member, security guard, or call for help.

Staying civil does not mean letting them walk all over you; it means you choose not to match rudeness with more rudeness, which usually only intensifies conflict.

---

## Managing Lines and Waiting Periods

Waiting in line is a common source of public anger—especially when the process is slow or disorganized. Some helpful tips:

1. **Enter With a Plan**
   Bring something to keep yourself occupied—a book, a puzzle on your phone, or a music playlist. This prevents your mind from fixating on how slow the line is.

2. **Practice Acceptance**
   Remind yourself, "I cannot speed up this line. Getting mad will not make it move faster." Acceptance can reduce futile anger.
3. **Break Tasks Into Steps**
   If it is a very long wait, you might aim to get past the next small milestone—like reaching the next section of the line. This can create a sense of small progress.
4. **Use Self-Talk**
   If your thoughts turn to, "They are wasting my time," switch to, "I have a few minutes to breathe and think. It is okay." Changing your inner voice lowers tension.
5. **Stay Polite to Staff**
   If you feel irritated, avoid snapping at the employees. They might not have control over the pace. Being rude to them often leads to more negativity.

Patience is a skill. Each time you resist blowing up in line, you strengthen your ability to stay calm under frustrating conditions.

---

## Handling Crowded Public Transport

Trains, buses, or subways can be cramped, noisy, and full of unexpected delays. To manage anger in these spaces:

1. **Time Your Commute**
   If possible, avoid peak rush hours. Even a 15-minute shift might mean fewer crowds.
2. **Create a Private Bubble**
   Headphones can block out chatter or loud announcements. Listening to a calming audio or quiet music can help you ignore minor irritations.
3. **Stand or Sit with Intention**
   If you feel trapped, try standing near a door so you can exit easily at your stop. If sitting, pick a seat that gives you some space, if available.
4. **Offer Kindness**
   Doing a small courtesy (like letting someone else get a seat) can shift your mindset from frustration to cooperation. This does not solve all problems, but a small act of kindness can calm your own irritability.

5. **Plan for Delays**
   Public transport can be late. Assume you might face a delay. Then, if it happens, it will not feel like such a shock, and your anger is less likely to flare.

A bit of forethought can turn a tense commute into a bearable or even peaceful experience.

---

## Social Events and Public Gatherings

Large social events—parties, concerts, or festivals—can trigger anger if you feel overwhelmed or stressed by certain personalities or unexpected drama:

1. **Set Boundaries**
   If a certain relative always starts arguments, decide ahead how long you will stay or how you will politely excuse yourself if they begin pushing your buttons.
2. **Take Breaks**
   Find a quiet corner, step outside for fresh air, or go to the restroom to breathe for a minute if you feel tension climbing.
3. **Stay Hydrated and Fed**
   At crowded events, it is easy to skip eating or drinking enough water. Low energy and dehydration can fuel anger.
4. **Choose Company Wisely**
   If you can, spend time with supportive friends or family at the event. A positive companion can buffer you from triggers.
5. **Have a Back-Up Exit Plan**
   Drive yourself or arrange a flexible ride, so if things become too heated, you have the freedom to leave.

Taking care of your emotional comfort at social events can reduce the risk of public outbursts.

---

## Minimizing Anger Online in Public Spaces

Modern life often mixes the digital world with the physical one. You might be in a café, scrolling through social media, and come across posts that enrage you:

1. **Limit Content That Upsets You**
   If you know reading certain topics or comments sets you off, avoid them while you are out and about. You will have fewer ways to calm down if your anger spikes in a public setting.
2. **Avoid Heated Online Arguments**
   Arguing on social media while sitting in a public space can distract you from your surroundings and raise your stress level. If a comment makes you angry, wait until you are in a calmer private setting to decide how to respond, if at all.
3. **Use the "Mute" or "Block" Features**
   If someone's online posts or messages always trigger anger, remove them from your feed or block them. You have the right to protect your peace.
4. **Pick Uplifting Content**
   Instead of doom scrolling, follow pages or people who post encouraging, funny, or helpful things. Fill your screen with positivity rather than triggers.

By controlling your online consumption in public spaces, you minimize digital triggers that can lead to real-life frustration.

---

## Helping Children Stay Calm in Public

If you have children with you, their behavior might add to your stress in public. Dealing with a child's meltdown can raise your own anger. Some suggestions:

1. **Prepare Activities**
   Bring small toys, coloring items, or snacks to keep them occupied. Bored children often act out, which can lead to your anger.
2. **Set Expectations**
   Before going out, let them know the plan and any rules. "We will stand in line calmly. If you feel restless, let me know, and we can do a quiet game."

3. **Stay Calm Yourself**
   Children model adults' emotions. If you keep your tone gentle, they are less likely to escalate.
4. **Plan Quick Breaks**
   If the child gets fussy, find a corner or quiet spot to settle them. This break also helps you breathe and regroup.
5. **Reward Quiet Patience**
   A simple nod or phrase—"Thank you for waiting without fussing"—can encourage them. Positive feedback for good behavior may lower your stress about them acting up.

When children behave better in public, you are less likely to feel anger building. A bit of foresight can make outings smoother for everyone.

---

## Responding to Criticism in Public

Sometimes, you might receive direct criticism or feedback in a public setting—maybe your boss calls you out in front of coworkers, or a stranger critiques your parenting style in a store:

1. **Check Your Reaction**
   Before you defend yourself or snap back, take a breath. Anger might tell you to argue loudly, but a calmer approach can save you from an embarrassing scene.
2. **Listen for Truth**
   Even if the criticism is delivered poorly, see if there is any truth in it. If yes, file it away to address later in private. If no, let it go.
3. **Stay Composed**
   Try a neutral reply: "I hear what you are saying," or "I appreciate your concern." End it there if the situation does not require further discussion.
4. **Move the Conversation Elsewhere**
   If it is important to address the criticism, suggest talking privately instead of in front of an audience.
5. **Know When to End the Exchange**
   If the critic keeps provoking you, politely excuse yourself. You do not have to stand there and keep absorbing unfair attacks.

By handling public criticism with composure, you avoid fueling further anger and show that you can maintain dignity under pressure.

## Exiting Gracefully

Sometimes the best solution is to remove yourself from a public setting that pushes your buttons:

1. **Scan Your Options**
   Where is the nearest exit, or can you walk to a calmer area? Are you free to leave right now, or do you need to finish an errand?
2. **Use a Calm Exit Phrase**
   If someone is pushing your anger, you might say, "I need a moment. Let's continue this later," or "I will step outside to catch my breath." This is more polite than storming out.
3. **Reward Yourself for Leaving Calmly**
   Once you are in a quieter place, note how you avoided a blow-up. A small internal pat on the back can reinforce your good choice.
4. **Reflect on the Situation**
   Later, think about what led to your decision to leave and whether there is a way to handle it differently if it happens again. This helps you prepare for future encounters.

Sometimes simply stepping away is the quickest route to preserving your peace.

## Self-Compassion After Public Tension

Even if you do your best to stay calm, you might still feel guilty if you get angry in public. Or you might be upset with yourself for not speaking up more. In both cases:

- **Acknowledge the Difficulty**: Public settings can be stressful. You are doing your best under tricky conditions.
- **Note Any Victories**: If you managed to keep your voice level or used a calming technique, that is progress.

- **Plan to Improve**: If you lost your temper, do not beat yourself up. Ask, "What can I do next time to handle it better?"
- **Treat Yourself Kindly**: A restful activity or gentle self-talk can help you bounce back from any lingering frustration.

Self-compassion helps you move on instead of lingering in shame or regret.

---

## Combining Public Calm with Overall Anger Management

The strategies in this book—understanding anger, safe expression, conflict resolution, relaxation, and forgiveness—can all apply to public situations:

- **Understanding**: Recognize you are not "bad" for feeling anger in public. You are facing unique stressors.
- **Expression**: If you must address a problem, do so calmly and respectfully.
- **Conflict Resolution**: If a public argument arises, try to keep lines of communication open but brief.
- **Relaxation**: Use quick breathing or grounding exercises whenever tension spikes.
- **Forgiveness**: If a stranger or event upset you, choose not to carry that resentment home with you. Let it go for your own peace.

Public calm is not separate from your overall anger management approach. It is simply another area where you apply these skills.

---

# Chapter 20: Making Long-Lasting Changes

Reaching the end of this book does not mean you have "finished" anger management. True growth is an ongoing process. You have explored many strategies: understanding anger, finding healthier outlets, communicating clearly, solving conflicts, practicing relaxation, and releasing anger through forgiveness. Now, the question is how to keep these changes strong in your life. In this concluding chapter, we will discuss how to create long-term habits, handle setbacks, and keep evolving so that anger does not overshadow your happiness.

## The Nature of Lasting Change

Change that endures is more than a single action—it becomes part of your daily routine. Think of it like building a house:

1. **Foundation**: Your basic understanding of anger—why it arises and what it signals.
2. **Walls**: The core skills you learned: safe expression, self-awareness, communication, etc.
3. **Roof**: Additional supports, like stress management and forgiveness, that protect you from being overwhelmed.
4. **Maintenance**: Regular checks to ensure nothing is weakening. If a crack appears, you fix it before it spreads.

Rather than seeing anger management as a one-time fix, view it as maintaining a strong house you can live in safely. Each new skill is part of that structure.

## Building Daily Routines

A lasting change often hinges on regular habits. Some examples:

1. **Morning Check-In**
   Soon after waking, spend a minute scanning your mood. If you sense tension, use a brief relaxation or grounding exercise. This prevents anger from sneaking up on you later.

2. **Scheduled Breaks**
   If you find that you get irritable by midday, plan a quick break. Stand up, stretch, or walk outside. These small pauses help keep stress from piling up.
3. **Daily Reflection**
   Before bed, ask yourself, "Did I face any anger triggers today? How did I respond? What worked, and what can I improve?" Write a short note in a journal or think about it quietly.
4. **Regular Self-Care**
   Rely on core practices—like exercise, healthy eating, and proper sleep—that form a base for emotional balance. If you let self-care slide, anger can creep back more easily.

By weaving these habits into everyday life, you reinforce your anger management skills so they become second nature.

---

## Setting Measurable Goals

Just saying "I want to be calmer" is broad. To track progress, define clear goals:

- **Example**: "I will pause and take three deep breaths each time I feel anger in the morning."
- **Example**: "I will walk away from an argument before shouting, at least twice this week."
- **Example**: "I will forgive myself for a past mistake by writing a letter to myself and letting go of guilt."

When you have specific targets, you can see concrete improvements. This progress keeps you motivated to continue, rather than slipping back into old habits.

---

## Handling Setbacks and Slips

No matter how strong your plan, you might slip into old patterns. Maybe you yell at a family member or lash out in traffic. These setbacks do not erase your progress. They are part of the process. Here is how to handle them:

1. **Stay Calm**
   Avoid beating yourself up. Harsh self-criticism can fuel more anger or shame.
2. **Review the Situation**
   Ask, "What triggered me? Was I tired, hungry, or stressed?" Understanding the cause helps you prevent future repeats.
3. **Offer an Apology or Repair**
   If your slip hurt someone, a sincere apology can mend trust. Promise yourself and them that you are still committed to growing.
4. **Adjust Your Strategy**
   Maybe your relaxation technique needs more practice, or you need to set stronger boundaries. Use the slip as a lesson to refine your approach.
5. **Reaffirm Your Commitment**
   Remind yourself that one setback does not define you. You are still on the path to healthier anger management.

Slips can actually deepen your learning. They highlight areas to strengthen, guiding you toward a steadier approach next time.

---

## Tracking Your Growth Over Time

Seeing evidence of improvement encourages you to keep going. You might:

- **Keep an Anger Log**
  Note each episode of anger, the trigger, your response, and the outcome. Over weeks or months, you can look back and see fewer outbursts or a calmer approach.
- **Ask Trusted Friends or Family**
  They might notice that you handle stress better or argue less often. Honest feedback from others can confirm your progress.

Tracking growth in small ways shows you that change is real and keeps you inspired to keep improving.

## Strengthening Key Relationships

Anger management often involves nurturing better relationships:

1. **Ongoing Communication**
   Keep practicing assertive but respectful dialogue with loved ones. This might mean scheduling a regular talk with your partner to discuss issues calmly or checking in with a friend after a tense exchange.
2. **Share Your Progress**
   Let family and close friends know how you are working on anger. If they see your efforts, they can support you and remind you of your skills when stress hits.
3. **Encourage Two-Way Respect**
   If someone notices you are slipping into anger, they might gently say, "Should we take a quick break?" Welcome their help, and likewise, respect their own emotional boundaries.
4. **Resolve Old Grudges**
   If there are lingering resentments, consider using conflict resolution or forgiveness approaches to clear the air. Unspoken hurts can become triggers later on.

Growing healthier patterns within key relationships builds a supportive environment that helps you maintain your calm over the long haul.

---

## Expanding Your Toolbox

Even after finishing this book, you can keep learning:

1. **Read More**
   Explore other books or articles on emotional wellness, conflict resolution, or mindfulness.
2. **Join a Class or Group**
   A local workshop on communication skills, a yoga class for stress relief, or an online support group can reinforce your anger management path.
3. **Professional Help**
   If deeper issues arise—such as trauma or intense mood swings—do not hesitate to talk to a therapist. They can tailor solutions to your specific needs.
4. **Try New Methods**
   Maybe you have never tried journaling or a certain relaxation method.

Experiment with fresh ideas to see what resonates best at different stages of your life.

As you add fresh tools, your ability to handle anger becomes more flexible. You can adapt to new challenges without reverting to old habits.

---

## Staying Mindful of Triggering Situations

Triggers can evolve as your life changes. Perhaps you start a new job or move to a different city. Keep an eye on how your environment shifts:

1. **Re-Evaluate Old Triggers**
   Something that once made you angry might no longer matter, while a new stressor could replace it.
2. **Update Boundaries**
   If your circle of friends changes or your responsibilities grow, you might need stronger boundaries around your time or emotional energy.
3. **Maintain Self-Awareness**
   Pay attention to your body's signals. If you feel tension creeping in, ask what is new or different in your life. Sometimes small changes—like a change in commute or a new coworker—can create hidden stress.
4. **Stay Flexible**
   Life is not static. Be ready to adjust your anger management strategies to fit new triggers or personal goals.

This ongoing mindfulness ensures you do not become complacent, letting anger slip back unnoticed.

---

## Keeping Balanced Expectations

Expecting zero anger forever is unrealistic. Anger will still show up sometimes, because it is part of being human. What changes is how you respond:

- **Accept Occasional Upset**: Feeling upset does not mean you failed. Anger can be a normal reaction when something is unfair or threatening.

- **Assess Its Use**: Before letting anger take over, ask: "Does expressing it this way help, or is there a healthier approach?"
- **Return to Your Skills**: Use the communication, relaxation, and boundary-setting methods you have learned.

Healthy anger management means letting anger alert you to problems while not letting it harm your well-being or relationships.

---

## Forgiveness and Calm as Ongoing Choices

From earlier chapters, you know forgiveness is not a one-time act, and calmness in public or private settings requires repeated effort. Remind yourself:

1. **Forgiveness May Need Renewing**
   Old hurts can resurface. That does not mean you never truly forgave. It just means you might need to reaffirm your choice to let go of resentment.
2. **Calm Takes Practice**
   In highly stressful phases, you might rely more on relaxation exercises or safe outlets for anger. As stress eases, you might find you need them less.
3. **Emotions Are Not Linear**
   You might have a wonderful month with little anger and then face a tough week. This is normal. Having tools ready ensures you handle that tough week gracefully.

By seeing forgiveness and calmness as repeating choices, you free yourself from the pressure of being "perfect" in anger management.

---

## Acknowledging Personal Victories

When you see positive changes in your anger response, give yourself credit. This encourages your brain to keep building those good habits. You might:

- **Record a Quick Note**: "I responded politely to a rude person in line today!" or "I felt angry but used deep breathing to calm down."

- **Share with a Supportive Friend**: Telling someone, "Hey, I did not snap at traffic at all this week," can reinforce your accomplishment.
- **Reflect on How It Felt**: Notice the relief or pride in staying calm. Let that feeling sink in, so your mind links calm responses with positive feelings.

Recognizing your own progress reminds you that your efforts matter and that change is happening.

---

## Handling Major Life Shifts

Major life changes—such as a job loss, a new baby, a move, or health issues—can test your anger management. To stay on track:

1. **Accept Extra Stress**
   During big shifts, stress is natural. Telling yourself you "should not" feel overwhelmed only adds more strain.
2. **Use Support**
   Lean on friends, family, or professional counselors. Let them know you are navigating a major change and might need a bit more understanding or help.
3. **Keep Up Core Routines**
   If possible, maintain the key routines—like daily breathing exercises or morning reflection—that have kept your anger in check.
4. **Adjust Goals**
   A new parent might not have time for a full 30-minute relaxation session daily. A 5-minute calm-down moment might become the new realistic goal. That is still progress.

Major life changes can derail you if you refuse to adapt. With flexible strategies, you can carry your anger management skills into each new phase.

---

## Sharing Your Knowledge

As you grow more confident in handling anger, you can share what you have learned:

- **Support a Friend**
  If a friend is dealing with anger, offer tips that worked for you, like deep breathing or "I" statements in conflicts.
- **Model Healthy Anger to Children**
  Show kids how to handle anger with calm words. This can shape them into adults who manage anger well, too.
- **Encourage a Partner**
  If your partner struggles with rage, invite them to try some exercises with you. A team effort can strengthen a relationship.

Sharing does not mean lecturing or forcing others to follow your path. It means offering gentle guidance if they are open. Teaching also reinforces your own habits.

## When to Seek More Help

You might be doing well overall, but certain deeper issues—like severe trauma, persistent shame, or patterns in your family—could need professional attention. Signs you might want extra help include:

- **Anger that still feels uncontrollable**
- **Harmful or violent urges**
- **Ongoing emotional pain from past events**
- **Trouble building healthy relationships even with your skills**
- **Physical or mental health concerns linked to stress**

Therapists, counselors, or anger management groups can provide deeper healing. Seeking help does not mean you failed. It means you are proactive in finding the best support for continued growth.

## Looking Back at Your Progress

Reflect on where you started. Maybe anger used to dominate your life more often. Now, you have new tools—breathing exercises, communication skills, conflict resolution steps, boundary-setting, trigger management, and forgiveness. You might notice:

- Less frequent outbursts
- Shorter anger episodes
- Better conversations with loved ones
- Greater sense of control and self-respect

Even if you are not "perfectly calm" all the time, these improvements show genuine change. Let that motivate you to stay on this path.

---

## Your Ongoing Growth

This book has been a guide, but your journey continues. You can keep building on these foundations, refining your approach, and discovering new ways to handle anger without letting it harm you or your relationships. Each challenge life brings can be another chance to practice what you have learned. Over time, you can develop a life marked by steadiness, understanding, and self-trust—where anger is a manageable signal rather than an overpowering force.

---

## Final Thoughts

Anger can be an alert that something matters to you: fairness, respect, safety, or love. When you manage anger wisely, you honor those values without letting anger drive you into actions you regret. By combining self-awareness, healthy outlets, communication, stress reduction, and forgiveness, you shape a way of living that respects both your feelings and the well-being of those around you.

Remember, you are not alone in this growth. Many women strive to handle anger better, and each step you take can inspire someone else to do the same. Keep practicing these skills, and do not lose heart if setbacks happen. Lasting change is possible when you commit to learning, adapting, and believing in your ability to guide anger instead of being guided by it. Here's to a life where frustration does not hold you back—but instead leads you to solutions, stronger connections, and a healthier sense of self.

www.ingramcontent.com/pod-product-compliance
Lightning Source LLC
LaVergne TN
LVHW012105070526
838202LV00056B/5625